200 cupcakes

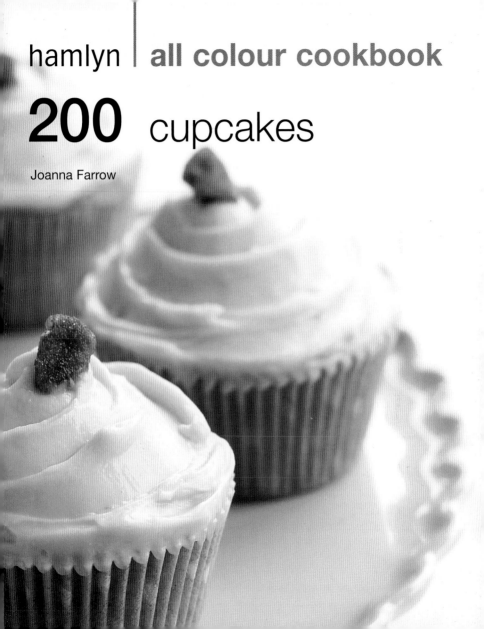

hamlyn | all colour cookbook

200 cupcakes

Joanna Farrow

An Hachette UK Company
www.hachette.co.uk

First published in Great Britain in 2010 by Hamlyn,
a division of Octopus Publishing Group Ltd,
Endeavour House, 189 Shaftesbury Avenue,
London WC2H 8JY
www.octopusbooks.co.uk

ISBN: 978-0-600-62078-5

A CIP catalogue record for this book is available from the
British Library

Printed and bound in China

7 8 9 10

Both metric and imperial measurements are given for the
recipes. Use one set of measures only, not a mixture of both.

Standard level spoon measures are used in all recipes:
1 tablespoon = one 15 ml spoon
1 teaspoon = one 5 ml spoon

Ovens should be preheated to the specified temperature.
If using a fan-assisted oven, follow the manufacturer's
instructions for adjusting the time and temperature.

Eggs should be medium unless otherwise stated; choose
free-range if possible and preferably organic. The Department
of Health advises that eggs should not be consumed raw.
This book contains some dishes made with raw or lightly
cooked eggs. It is prudent for more vulnerable people, such
as pregnant and nursing mothers, invalids, the elderly, babies
and young children, to avoid uncooked or lightly cooked
dishes made with eggs.

This book includes dishes made with nuts and nut
derivatives. It is advisable for those with known allergic
reactions to nuts and nut derivatives and those who may be
potentially vulnerable to these allergies, such as pregnant and
nursing mothers, invalids, the elderly, babies and children, to
avoid dishes made with nuts and nut oils. It is also prudent to
check the labels of prepared ingredients for the possible
inclusion of nut derivatives.

contents

introduction   6

everyday cupcakes   20

chocolate cupcakes   68

cupcakes for kids   104

cupcakes for adults   142

savoury cupcakes   180

special occasion cupcakes   202

index   234

acknowledgements   240

introduction

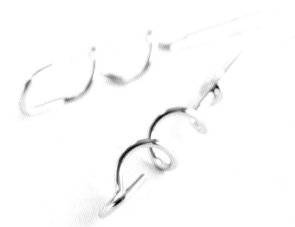

introduction

Cupcakes have become very popular in recent years, and it's easy to see why. Each little cake, with its soft, spongy base and sweet topping, provides the perfect-sized portion for an indulgent treat. Cupcakes also have both child and adult appeal. Kids love helping both to make and decorate them, and their enthusiasm for doing so never seems to flag. Conveniently packaged in their mini paper cases, cupcakes are incredibly versatile – ideal for any occasion from everyday tea to a special-occasion party. Above all, cupcakes are so effortless to make. While a simple glacé icing is just

the thing for teatime, you may want to try something a little more impressive if you've got friends coming over, or if you have a kid's birthday tea to cater for or would like to take a selection as a gift or to share, beautifully boxed, when you next visit friends or family.

cupcakes for special occasions

The trend for cupcakes to take the place of a large, traditionally iced cake for a special occasion is becoming an increasingly favoured option. The big bonus here is that they can be attempted by anyone, experienced or beginner, without the need to order them from a specialist supplier. For example, a stunning array of the Wedding Cupcakes on page 224 would look spectacular presented on a tiered cupcake stand (see opposite), while other prettily decorated cupcakes would make an impressive centrepiece for a major birthday, anniversary or almost any other celebration. Decorations can be as simple as fresh fruit or bought sugar flowers, or if you've the time and inclination, sugared fresh flowers (see page 228) or other finishing touches. All look equally impressive. In the book you will also find seasonal flavours and decorations that are perfectly suited to Christmas, Easter and Halloween (see pages 204–223).

equipment

Cupcakes require only basic equipment. For most of the recipes, a bun or muffin tray, paper cake cases and a hand-held electric whisk is all that's needed to make a batch of delicious cakes, ready for decorating as simply or creatively as you like.

bun trays

These vary slightly, but are usually about the size that you'd use for baking individual jam tarts. The sections generally have sloping sides and are also available with a nonstick coating, which is useful if you're making little cakes without paper cases.

muffin trays

This type of tray has larger, deeper sections with straighter sides, ideal for making larger cupcakes for adult-sized portions. Muffin trays are also available with a nonstick coating.

paper cake cases

These come in a vast range of sizes from tiny 'fairy cake' cases for kids' cakes to giant-sized muffin ones. There's also a feast of colours and designs to choose from. Look out for novelty designs for children's birthdays, as well as gold, silver and coloured foils for festive cakes and a rainbow of other hues, from pale pastels to vivid reds. Most of the recipes in this book are designed for a paper case that's larger than a fairy cake case, but smaller than a muffin one. Use whichever size you prefer, though of course if using a muffin case where a cake case is called for you won't make as many, and visa versa. A couple of the recipes in the book use mini paper cake cases, sometimes sold as 'petit four' cases. Tins with tiny holes are available, but you can position the cases directly on a baking sheet.

silicone cases

Brightly coloured or pastel-shaded silicone cupcake cases are great for a reliable supply and can even be bought in heart or other novelty shapes. Reusable and dishwasher-proof as well as ovenproof, they're easy to use and can be positioned on a baking sheet for cooking rather than in tin sections. After use, wash and dry thoroughly before storing.

cutters

Made out of metal or plastic, small cookie cutters, and even smaller cake-decorating cutters in flower or novelty shapes, are great for simple but effective decorations. They range from regular rounds to number and letter shapes, animals, stars, moons, trees and many seasonal motifs. Buy these when you see them and build up a collection in case you can't find them in the shops when the occasion arises.

cupcake stands

Whether for a birthday party or wedding celebration, piling up cupcakes on a tiered stand looks stunning and eliminates the need for cake cutting. These stands are available in easily assembled card or clear acetate with pillars or separators to create the layers. Metal cupcake stands that incorporate individual sections to support each cupcake are a good choice for smaller gatherings. Look in cook shops or specialist cake-decorating shops, or on the internet, for a variety of design options.

storing cupcakes

Cupcakes are best served freshly baked. However, if making ahead, they'll keep well in an airtight container for 24 hours, but if keeping them for more than a couple of days, it's best to freeze them, allowing them to thaw for several hours before decorating. Cakes decorated with buttercream or chocolate frosting such as the Coffee

& Walnut Cupcakes on page 170 or the Chocolate Fudge Cupcakes on page 70 can be frozen ready decorated, but those finished with whipped cream or icings are best decorated once thawed.

some simple techiques

Unlike larger cakes, which are more prone to sinking in the centre or being over- or undercooked, there's less that can go wrong when making cupcakes.

mixing the basic sponge

Most of the recipes use the 'all-in-one' method in which all the cake ingredients are beaten in a bowl using a hand-held electric whisk or using a free standing electric mixer.

Make sure you've softened the butter beforehand (either gently in a microwave oven or by letting it stand at room temperature) so that the mixture creams together easily. This will take about a minute using the whisk or three to four minutes if you're using a wooden spoon to mix. The ingredients can also be whizzed together in a large food processor.

making muffins

Muffins are made by folding the 'wet' ingredients, such as eggs, melted butter and buttermilk or milk, into the dry ingredients, including the flour, baking powder, dried fruits and flavourings. Use a large metal spoon and fold the ingredients gently together until they're only just combined. It doesn't matter if there are traces of flour dispersed in the mixture; overmixing the ingredients will produce a tougher texture.

filling the cases

Cake mixtures rise as they bake, so take care not to overfill the cases or the mixture will fall over the sides and make the sponge deflate. To avoid this, don't fill the cases more than about two-thirds full. If baking more than 12 cakes, or if you have excess mixture and are not using a fan oven, bake in two separate batches rather than rotating the trays halfway through cooking as you might with cookies or meringues, since opening the oven halfway through cooking will make the cakes deflate.

testing whether the cakes are cooked

At the end of the cooking time, gently open the oven and lightly touch the top of one of the cakes. The cakes should have risen and the surface should feel soft but not give to the touch. For a basic sponge mixture the crust should be pale golden. Avoid overcooking or the cakes will taste dry.

cooling the cakes

Most of the cupcakes are cooled before decorating. Leave them in the tin for a couple of minutes once you have taken them out of the oven, then carefully lift them on to a wire rack. Leave until completely cold before decorating, particularly if using whipped cream or buttercream. Some cakes, including the muffin recipes and savoury cupcakes, are best served warm to enjoy their flavour at its best. Muffins don't keep well and any leftovers should be warmed through to refresh them before serving. Ideally, any that are not eaten freshly baked should be frozen for later use.

piped decorations

Ingredients such as whipped cream, meringue, melted chocolate and buttercream can be piped on to cupcakes for a more formal, uniform presentation rather than simply spooning or spreading with a knife. Reusable nylon piping bags, available from specialist cake-decorating shops or cook shops, can be fitted with a star or plain piping nozzle for piping and then washed ready for reusing. These are good for piping large swirls or

decorations on to cakes such as the Coffee & Walnut Cupcakes on page 170.

For piping scribbled lines or more intricate decorations, such as the Piped Shell Cupcakes on page 30, a paper piping bag is an easier option. These can be bought ready made from good cake-decorating suppliers or you can make your own from triangles of greaseproof paper (see page 16). The advantage of using a disposable bag is that you can have several different bags in use at one time, for example when using different-coloured icings for decoration. It also means that you can snip off the merest tip of the bag for piping without having to insert a plastic or metal nozzle. Take care not to snip off too much of the tip or the icing will flow out too thick and fast.

making a paper piping bag

Cut out a 25 cm (10 inch) square of greaseproof paper. Fold it diagonally in half. Cut the paper in half, just to one side of the folded line. Holding one piece with the long edge away from you, curl the right-hand point over to meet the centre point, making a cone shape. Bring the left-hand point over the cone so the three points meet. Fold the points over several times to secure the cone. Snip off the tip and insert a piping nozzle, if using. Half fill the bag and fold over the end to secure.

writing icing

Tubes of writing icing can be bought in many colours as a quick and easy cake decoration. Some come with changeable tips for piping.

melting chocolate

There are three ways of melting chocolate. When melted with butter or milk, the melting time will be reduced because of the high fat content of these additional ingredients.

To melt on the hob, chop the chocolate into small pieces and put in a heatproof bowl. Set the bowl over a saucepan of gently simmering water, making sure the base of the bowl doesn't come in contact with the water. Once the chocolate starts to melt, turn off the heat and leave until completely melted, stirring once or twice until no lumps remain. It's crucial that no water (including steam) gets into the bowl or the chocolate will solidify and can't be melted again.

To melt in a microwave oven, chop the chocolate into small pieces and put in a microwave-proof bowl. Melt the chocolate in one-minute spurts, checking frequently. Take particular care when melting white or milk chocolate, as they have a higher sugar content and are more prone to scorching.

To melt in the oven, chop the chocolate into small pieces and put in a small ovenproof dish or bowl. Put in the switched-off oven after baking and leave until melted.

using ready-to-roll icing
This soft, pliable icing is available from supermarkets, usually in white or basic colours, or in a wider range of colours from specialist

cake-decorating shops or suppliers. It can be rolled out on a surface lightly dusted with icing sugar and cut into shapes using cutters or moulded like plasticine into shapes. If opening a new slab of ready-to-roll icing, knead it lightly to soften it up before rolling out. White icing can be coloured by kneading in a few drops of liquid food colouring (to a pastel shade) or paste colouring (for a stronger shade). Any icing that's not in use should be wrapped tightly in clingfilm to prevent it drying out.

using ready-made decorations
These can range from supermarket-bought sugar sprinkles, tiny sweets and chocolates through to handmade edible flowers available from specialist cake-decorating shops or

17

suppliers. You may want to check the ingredients used in some of the cheaper bought decorations before you decide to buy them, or at least use them very sparingly.

frostings

The following favourite frostings are used in several recipes in the book. Alternatively, use them as fillings or toppings for other cupcake recipes of your choice. All three frostings are quick and easy to make but the chocolate fudge frostings take a little longer, as the chocolate needs to be melted.

buttercream

Makes **enough to generously cover 12 cupcakes**
Preparation time **5 minutes**

150 g (5 oz) **unsalted butter**, softened
250 g (8 oz) **icing sugar**
1 teaspoon **vanilla extract**
2 teaspoons **hot water**

Put the butter and icing sugar in a bowl and beat well with a wooden spoon or hand-held electric whisk until smooth and creamy.

Add the vanilla extract and hot water and beat again until smooth.

chocolate fudge frosting

Makes **enough to cover 12 cupcakes**
Preparation time **5 minutes**
Cooking time **5 minutes**

100 g (3½ oz) **plain** or **milk chocolate**, chopped
2 tablespoons **milk**
50 g (2 oz) **unsalted butter**
75 g (3 oz) **icing sugar**

Put the chocolate, milk and butter in a small, heavy-based saucepan and heat gently, stirring, until the chocolate and butter have melted.

Remove from the heat and stir in the icing sugar until smooth. Spread the frosting over the tops of cupcakes while still warm.

white chocolate fudge frosting

Makes **enough to cover 12 cupcakes**
Preparation time **5 minutes**
Cooking time **5 minutes**

200 g (7 oz) **white chocolate**, chopped
5 tablespoons **milk**
175 g (6 oz) **icing sugar**

Put the chocolate and milk in a heatproof bowl. Set the bowl over a saucepan of very gently simmering water and leave until melted, stirring frequently.

Remove the bowl from the pan and stir in the icing sugar until smooth. Spread the frosting over the tops of cupcakes while still warm.

everyday
cupcakes

vanilla cupcakes

Makes **12**
Preparation time **10 minutes**
Cooking time **20 minutes**

150 g (5 oz) **lightly salted
  butter**, softened
150 g (5 oz) **caster sugar**
175 g (6 oz) **self-raising flour**
3 **eggs**
1 teaspoon **vanilla extract**

Line a 12-section bun tray with paper or foil cake cases, or stand 12 silicone cases on a baking sheet. Put all the cake ingredients in a bowl and beat with a hand-held electric whisk for 1–2 minutes until light and creamy. Divide the cake mixture between the paper, foil or silicone cases.

Bake in a preheated oven, 180°C (350°F), Gas Mark 4, for 20 minutes or until risen and just firm to the touch. Transfer to a wire rack to cool.

For cranberry spice cupcakes, make the cake mixture as above, but add ½ teaspoon ground mixed spice and 1 piece of stem ginger from a jar, finely chopped, to the cake ingredients before beating. Once beaten, stir in 75 g (3 oz) dried cranberries. Bake as above.

For chocolate cupcakes, make the cake mixture as above, but substitute 15 g (½ oz) cocoa powder for 15 g (½ oz) of the flour.

fruit & nut cupcakes

Makes **18**
Preparation time **10 minutes**
Cooking time **25 minutes**

150 g (5 oz) **lightly salted
    butter**, softened
150 g (5 oz) **light
    muscovado sugar**
200 g (7 oz) **self-raising flour**
3 **eggs**
1 teaspoon **almond extract**
50 g (2 oz) **chopped mixed
    nuts**
75 g (3 oz) **mixed dried fruit**

Line 2 x 12-section bun trays with 18 paper cake cases. Put the butter, sugar, flour, eggs and almond extract in a bowl and beat with a hand-held electric whisk for 1–2 minutes until light and creamy.

Add the chopped nuts and dried fruit and stir until evenly combined. Divide the cake mixture between the paper cases.

Bake in a preheated oven, 180°C (350°F), Gas Mark 4, for 25 minutes or until risen and just firm to the touch. Transfer to a wire rack to cool.

For date & orange cupcakes, take 150 g (5 oz) plump stoned dried dates. Cut 6 lengthways into thin slices and chop the remainder. Make the cake mixture as above, but use the finely grated rind of 1 orange in place of the almond extract and add the chopped dates instead of the fruit and nuts. Arrange the date slices over the cakes before baking as above.

carrot cupcakes

Makes **12**

Preparation time **20 minutes**, plus cooling

Cooking time **25 minutes**

150 g (5 oz) **lightly salted butter**, softened

150 g (5 oz) **light muscovado sugar**

3 **eggs**

150 g (5 oz) **self-raising flour**

½ teaspoon **baking powder**

1 teaspoon **ground mixed spice**

75 g (3 oz) **ground walnuts**

finely grated **rind** of 1 **orange**

150 g (5 oz) **carrots**, grated

50 g (2 oz) **sultanas**

Frosting

125 g (4 oz) **full-fat cream cheese**

275 g (9 oz) **icing sugar**

1 tablespoon **lemon juice**

chopped **walnuts**, to decorate

Line a 12-section muffin tray with paper muffin cases. Put the butter, muscovado sugar, eggs, flour, baking powder, mixed spice, ground walnuts and orange rind in a bowl and beat with a hand-held electric whisk for about a minute until light and creamy.

Stir in the grated carrots and sultanas until evenly mixed. Divide the cake mixture between the paper cases.

Bake in a preheated oven, 180°C (350°F), Gas Mark 4, for 25 minutes or until risen and just firm to the touch. Leave in the tin for 5 minutes, then transfer to a wire rack to cool.

Beat the cream cheese in a bowl with a wooden spoon until smooth and creamy. Beat in the icing sugar and lemon juice. Spread over the tops of the cakes using a small palette knife and scatter with chopped walnuts to decorate.

For courgette & hazelnut cupcakes, grate 150 g (5 oz) courgettes and put in a small colander. Sprinkle with 2 teaspoons salt and stir together. Put on a plate and leave to stand for 30 minutes. Rinse thoroughly in several changes of cold water to remove all traces of salt. Pat dry between several sheets of kitchen paper. Make the cake mixture as above, but use 75 g (3 oz) ground hazelnuts in place of the ground walnuts and stir in the grated courgettes instead of the grated carrots with the sultanas. Make the frosting as above and spread over the cakes, then scatter with chopped hazelnuts.

marbled coffee cupcakes

Makes **12**
Preparation time **15 minutes**
Cooking time **20 minutes**

125 g (4 oz) **lightly salted butter**, softened
125 g (4 oz) **caster sugar**, plus 2 teaspoons
2 **eggs**
150 g (5 oz) **self-raising flour**
½ teaspoon **baking powder**
2 teaspoons **espresso coffee powder**
1 teaspoon boiling water
50 g (2 oz) **flaked almonds**, lightly toasted
¼ teaspoon **ground cinnamon**

Line a 12-section bun tray with paper cake cases. Put the butter, the 125 g (4 oz) sugar, eggs, flour and baking powder in a bowl and beat with a hand-held electric whisk for about a minute until light and creamy.

Spoon half the cake mixture into a separate bowl. Blend the coffee powder with the boiling water and stir into half the mixture. Using a teaspoon, fill the paper cases with the 2 mixtures, then draw a knife in a circular motion through each cupcake to mix the mixtures partially together to create a marbled effect.

Scatter the flaked almonds over the cakes. Mix the remaining 2 teaspoons sugar with the cinnamon and sprinkle over the cakes.

Bake in a preheated oven, 180°C (350°F), Gas Mark 4, for 20 minutes or until risen and just firm to the touch. Transfer to a wire rack to cool.

For rippled raspberry cupcakes, make the cake mixture as above. Crush 75 g (3 oz) fresh raspberries in a bowl with 2 teaspoons caster sugar so that they are broken up but not turning to a juicy mush. Half fill the paper cases with the cake mixture and flatten with the back of a spoon. Divide the raspberry mixture between the cases and top with the remaining cake mixture. Bake as above and serve dusted with icing sugar.

piped shell cupcakes

Makes **12**

Preparation time **40 minutes**, plus cooling

Cooking time **20 minutes**

200 g (7 oz) **icing sugar**, plus a little extra

1–2 tablespoons **lemon** or **orange juice**

12 **Vanilla Cupcakes** (see page 22)

½ quantity **Buttercream** (see page 18)

a few drops of **pink** and **lilac food colouring**

Mix the sugar with 1 tablespoon of the lemon or orange juice in a bowl. Gradually add the remaining juice, stirring well with a wooden spoon, until the icing holds its shape but is not difficult to spread – you may not need all the juice.

Reserve 3 tablespoons of the icing and spread the remainder over the tops of the cooled cakes using a small palette knife. Stir a little extra sugar into the reserved icing to thicken it until it just forms peaks when lifted with a knife. Put in a piping bag fitted with a writing nozzle, or use a paper piping bag with the merest tip snipped off (see page 15).

Colour half the buttercream with pink food colouring and the other half with lilac food colouring. Put in separate piping bags fitted with star nozzles.

Pipe rows of pink and lilac buttercream and white icing across the cakes.

For sweetheart cupcakes, press a 3–4 cm (1¼–1¾ inch) heart-shaped cutter down about 5 mm (¼ inch) into each cupcake and lift out. Scoop out the heart shape. Melt 6 tablespoons strawberry or raspberry jam in a saucepan until softened and spoon into the cavities, spreading it to the edges. Make a small quantity of buttercream by beating together 25 g (1 oz) softened unsalted butter with 50 g (2 oz) icing sugar and put in a paper piping bag fitted with a writing nozzle. Use to pipe an outline around the edge of each heart shape.

double berry muffins

Makes **12**
Preparation time **10 minutes**
Cooking time **20 minutes**

300 g (10 oz) **plain flour**
3 teaspoons **baking powder**
125 g (4 oz) **caster sugar**
50 g (2 oz) **lightly salted
  butter**
3 **eggs**
4 tablespoons **sunflower oil**
1½ teaspoons **vanilla extract**
150 g (5 oz) **natural yogurt**
100 g (3½ oz) **fresh
  blueberries**
100 g (3½ oz) **fresh
  raspberries**

Line a 12-section muffin tray with paper muffin cases.
Put the flour, baking powder and sugar in a bowl and
stir together using a fork.

Melt the butter in a small saucepan over a gentle heat
and then pour into the dry ingredients. Add the eggs,
oil, vanilla extract and yogurt and stir together until only
just combined. Stir in the fresh berries. Divide the
muffin mixture between the paper cases.

Bake in a preheated oven, 200°C (400°F), Gas Mark 6,
for 15 minutes or until the muffins are well risen and
the tops have cracked and turned golden brown.

Loosen the edges of the paper cases with a round-
bladed knife to serve warm or transfer to a wire rack
to cool.

For juniper & grapefruit muffins, cut away the rind
from 2 grapefruit. Working over a bowl to catch the
juice, cut the segments from between the membranes.
Cut the segments into small pieces. Grind 12 juniper
berries with 1 tablespoon caster sugar as finely as
possible in a mortar with a pestle. Make the muffin
mixture as above, but omit the berries and add the
juniper sugar to the dry ingredients and the grapefruit
pieces with the wet ingredients. Bake as above, then
drizzle with a glaze made by mixing 2 teaspoons
grapefruit juice with 50 g (2 oz) icing sugar.

lemon & lime drizzle cupcakes

Makes **12**
Preparation time **20 minutes**
Cooking time **35 minutes**

1 **lemon**
2 **limes**
150 g (5 oz) **lightly salted
  butter**, softened
200 g (7 oz) **caster sugar**
3 **eggs**
150 g (5 oz) **self-raising flour**
½ teaspoon **baking powder**
50 g (2 oz) **ground almonds**

Stand 12 silicone cake cases on a baking sheet, or line a 12-section bun tray with paper cases. Pare thin strips of rind from the lemon and one of the limes using a sharp knife. Slice the pared strips as finely as possible into shreds. Put them in a small saucepan and just cover with cold water. Cook very gently for about 15 minutes until the shreds are tender – they should be soft enough to break up when squeezed between your thumb and forefinger. Drain and leave to cool.

Squeeze the juice from the lemon and limes.

Put the butter, 150 g (5 oz) of the sugar, the eggs, flour, baking powder and ground almonds in a bowl. Beat with a hand-held electric whisk for about a minute until light and creamy. Divide the cake mixture between the silicone or paper cases.

Bake in a preheated oven, 180°C (350°F), Gas Mark 4, for 20 minutes or until risen and just firm to the touch. Transfer to a wire rack.

Scatter the rind over the cakes while still warm and drizzle with the juice. Sprinkle with the remaining sugar and leave to cool.

For orange & hazelnut drizzle cakes, pare the rind from 2 small oranges and squeeze 5 tablespoons of orange juice. Shred and cook the orange rind as above. Make the cake mixture as above, but use 50 g (2 oz) ground hazelnuts in place of the ground almonds. Bake as above. Once cooled, scatter the cakes with the drained orange rind shreds and 25 g (1 oz) chopped hazelnuts. Spoon over the orange juice and sprinkle with the remaining sugar as above.

warm pecan caramel cupcakes

Makes **12**

Preparation time **15 minutes**

Cooking time **25 minutes**

125 g (4 oz) **lightly salted butter**, softened

125 g (4 oz) **light muscovado sugar**

2 **eggs**

150 g (5 oz) **self-raising flour**

½ teaspoon **baking powder**

1 teaspoon **vanilla extract**

100 g (3½ oz) **pecan nuts**, roughly chopped

250 g (8 oz) **caramel sauce** (see right for homemade)

Line a 12-section bun tray with paper cake cases. Put the butter, sugar, eggs, flour, baking powder and vanilla extract in a bowl and beat with a hand-held electric whisk for about a minute until light and creamy.

Stir in three-quarters of the pecan nuts and then divide the cake mixture between the paper cases.

Bake in a preheated oven, 180°C (350°F), Gas Mark 4, for 20 minutes or until risen and just firm to the touch. Transfer to a wire rack.

Tip the caramel sauce into a small saucepan and stir gently over a medium heat until melted but not boiling. Drizzle the sauce over the cakes while still warm and scatter with the remaining pecan nuts. You may want to take the cakes out of their cases to serve.

For homemade caramel sauce, to drizzle over the cupcakes, put 200 g (7 oz) caster sugar in a small saucepan with 75 ml (3 fl oz) water and heat very gently, stirring, until the sugar has dissolved. Bring to the boil and boil rapidly, without stirring, until the syrup turns to a pale caramel colour (watch closely, as the syrup will quickly overbrown). Remove from the heat and stir in 50 g (2 oz) lightly salted butter and 150 ml (¼ pint) double cream. Return to the heat and cook, stirring, until smooth.

strawberry cream cupcakes

Makes **12**

Preparation time **30 minutes**, plus cooling

Cooking time **20 minutes**

12 **Vanilla Cupcakes** (see page 22)

300 g (10 oz) **small fresh strawberries**

150 ml (¼ pint) **double cream**

2 teaspoons **caster sugar**

½ teaspoon **vanilla extract**

4 tablespoons **redcurrant jelly**

1 tablespoon **water**

Scoop out the centre of each cooled cake using a small, sharp knife to leave a deep cavity in each cake.

Hull the strawberries and reserve 6 of the smallest. Thinly slice the remainder.

Whip the cream, sugar and vanilla extract with a hand-held electric whisk in a bowl until just peaking. Spoon a little into the centre of each cake and flatten slightly with the back of the spoon.

Arrange the sliced strawberries, overlapping, around the edges of each cake. Halve the reserved strawberries and place a strawberry half in the centre of each cake.

Heat the redcurrant jelly with the water in a small, heavy-based saucepan until melted, then brush over the strawberries using a pastry brush. Store the cakes in a cool place until ready to serve.

For banoffi cream cupcakes, make and bake the Vanilla Cupcakes as on page 22, but use 150 g (5 oz) light muscovado sugar instead of the caster sugar for the cake ingredients. Slice 2 small bananas and toss in 1 tablespoon lemon juice. Whip 150 ml (¼ pint) double cream with 1 teaspoon vanilla extract until just holding its shape. Place a spoonful on each cooled cake and spread to the edges with the back of a teaspoon. Spoon ½ tablespoon of shop-bought toffee sauce from a jar into the centre of each cake and scatter with the bananas. Crush a gingernut biscuit and scatter a little over each cake.

sultana & ginger cupcakes

Makes **12**

Preparation time **15 minutes**, plus cooling

Cooking time **20 minutes**

50 g (2 oz) piece of **fresh root ginger**

125 g (4 oz) **lightly salted butter**, softened

125 g (4 oz) **caster sugar**

2 **eggs**

150 g (5 oz) **self-raising flour**

½ teaspoon **baking powder**

½ teaspoon **vanilla extract**

50 g (2 oz) **sultanas**

200 g (7 oz) **icing sugar**

several pieces of **crystallized ginger**, very thinly sliced, to decorate

Line a 12-section bun tray with paper cake cases. Peel and finely grate the ginger, working over a plate to catch the juice. Put the butter, caster sugar, eggs, flour, baking powder and vanilla extract in a bowl. Add the grated ginger, reserving the juice for the icing. Beat with a hand-held electric whisk for about a minute until light and creamy.

Stir in the sultanas and then divide the cake mixture between the paper cases.

Bake in a preheated oven, 180°C (350°F), Gas Mark 4, for 20 minutes or until risen and just firm to the touch. Transfer to a wire rack to cool.

Beat the icing sugar in a bowl with the ginger juice, making up with enough water to create an icing that just holds its shape. Spread over the tops of the cakes with a small palette knife. Decorate with the crystallized ginger slices.

For butter-iced ginger cupcakes, make the cake mixture as above, but use 3 pieces of finely chopped stem ginger from a jar instead of the fresh ginger and then stir in 50 g (2 oz) thinly sliced stoned dried dates in place of the sultanas. Bake as above. Beat 100 g (3½ oz) softened unsalted butter with 175 g (6 oz) icing sugar and 1 teaspoon hot water until smooth and creamy. Spread over the tops of the cooled cakes and scatter with extra chopped stem ginger to decorate.

rose delight cupcakes

Makes **12**

Preparation time **15 minutes**, plus cooling

Cooking time **20 minutes**

125 g (4 oz) **rose-flavoured Turkish delight**

125 g (4 oz) **lightly salted butter**, softened

125 g (4 oz) **caster sugar**

2 **eggs**

150 g (5 oz) **self-raising flour**

½ teaspoon **baking powder**

1 teaspoon **vanilla extract**

Topping

300 ml (½ pint) **double cream**

2 teaspoons **rosewater**

2 teaspoons **icing sugar**

seeds of 1 small **pomegranate**

Line a 12-section bun tray with paper cake cases. Cut the Turkish delight into small pieces using scissors. Put all the remaining cake ingredients in a bowl and beat with a hand-held electric whisk for about a minute until light and creamy.

Stir in the Turkish delight and then divide the cake mixture between the paper cases.

Bake in a preheated oven, 180°C (350°F), Gas Mark 4, for 20 minutes or until risen and just firm to the touch. Transfer to a wire rack to cool.

Whip the cream in a bowl with the rosewater and icing sugar until just peaking. Swirl over the tops of the cakes with a small palette knife or pipe through a large star nozzle and scatter with the pomegranate seeds.

For sugar-dusted rose cupcakes, make the cake mixture as above, but omit the Turkish delight. Bake as above. Meanwhile, mix together 50 g (2 oz) caster sugar, 1 tablespoon rosewater and 2 teaspoons lemon juice. Pierce the cooked, still-warm cakes all over with a skewer and drizzle with the sugar mixture until absorbed. Leave to cool, then generously dust with icing sugar.

very cherry cupcakes

Makes **12**

Preparation time **20 minutes**, plus cooling

Cooking time **25 minutes**

100 g (3½ oz) **whole blanched almonds**

100 g (3½ oz) **lightly salted butter**, softened

100 g (3½ oz) **caster sugar**

2 **eggs**

125 g (4 oz) **self-raising flour**

1 teaspoon **baking powder**

100 g (3½ oz) **natural glacé cherries**, quartered

4 tablespoons **cherry** or **strawberry jam**

100 g (3½ oz) **icing sugar**

2–3 teaspoons **water**

6 **fresh cherries**, halved and stoned, to decorate

Line a 12-section bun tray with paper cake cases. Put the almonds in a food processor and process until ground.

Tip the ground almonds into a bowl and add the butter, caster sugar, eggs, flour and baking powder. Beat well using a hand-held electric whisk for about a minute until light and creamy.

Stir in the glacé cherries and then divide the cake mixture between the paper cases.

Bake in a preheated oven, 180°C (350°F), Gas Mark 4, for 25 minutes or until risen and just firm to the touch. Transfer to a wire rack to cool.

Press the jam through a sieve to remove any lumps and spread over the tops of the cakes. Beat the icing sugar in a bowl with the water to make a thick icing that almost holds its shape. Spread a little over each cake and decorate with the cherry halves.

For spicy pineapple cupcakes, make the cake mixture as above, but add ½ teaspoon ground ginger to the other ingredients before beating. Once beaten, stir in 100 g (3½ oz) semi-dried pineapple, chopped into small pieces, in place of the glacé cherries. Bake as above and leave to cool. Press 5 tablespoons pineapple or ginger jam through a sieve to remove any lumps and brush over the tops of the cakes. Scatter with 75 g (3 oz) crushed gingernut biscuits and dust with icing sugar to serve.

butterfly cupcakes

Makes **12**
Preparation time **25 minutes**,
  plus cooling
Cooking time **20 minutes**

12 **Vanilla Cupcakes**
  (see page 22)
1 quantity **Buttercream**
  (see page 18)

Cut out a round from the centre top of each cooled cake neatly using a small, sharp knife. Cut each round in half.

Put the buttercream in a big piping bag fitted with a large star nozzle. Pipe a large swirl of buttercream into the cavity of each cake.

Reposition the 2 halves of the rounds on each cake at an angle of 45° so that they resemble butterfly wings.

For vanilla custard butterfly cupcakes, beat together 4 egg yolks, 50 g (2 oz) caster sugar, 1 teaspoon vanilla extract and 15 g (½ oz) plain flour in a heatproof bowl. Bring 150 ml (¼ pint) double cream and 150 ml (¼ pint) milk to the boil in a small saucepan. Pour over the egg yolk mixture, stirring to mix. Return to the pan and cook over a gentle heat, stirring constantly, until very thick. Turn into a small bowl, sprinkle with sugar to prevent a skin forming and leave to cool. Follow the recipe above, but use the vanilla custard instead of the buttercream.

orange & lemon cupcakes

Makes **12**

Preparation time **20 minutes**,
plus cooling & setting

Cooking time **15–20 minutes**

50 g (2 oz) **lightly salted
butter**

100 g (3½ oz) **caster sugar**

2 **eggs**

100 g (3½ oz) **self-raising
flour**

1 tablespoon finely grated
lemon rind

2 tablespoons **orange
flower water**

2–3 tablespoons **milk**

Icing

200 g (7 oz) **icing sugar**,
sifted

1½ tablespoons **orange juice**

1½ tablespoons **lemon juice**

yellow and **orange food
colouring**

finely pared **orange** and
**lemon rind coated in
caster sugar**, to decorate

Line a 12-section muffin tray with paper or foil muffin cases. Put the butter, caster sugar, eggs, flour and grated lemon rind in a bowl and beat with a hand-held electric whisk until smooth.

Add the orange flower water and enough milk to give a good dropping consistency. Divide the cake mixture between the paper or foil cases.

Bake in a preheated oven, 200°C (400°F), Gas Mark 6, for 15–20 minutes or until risen and golden. Transfer to a wire rack to cool.

Slice the risen tops off the cakes. Mix half the icing sugar with the orange juice in one bowl and the other half with the lemon juice in another bowl. Dot a tiny amount of the relevant food colouring into each one and stir well until you have 2 pastel-coloured icings.

Pour a small amount of the orange icing over 6 of the cakes using a teaspoon to cover the surface evenly. Repeat with the remaining cakes, using the yellow icing. Decorate with the sugar-coated orange and lemon rind, pressing it on lightly. Leave to set completely.

For gooseberry & elderflower cupcakes, make the cake mixture as above, using 2 tablespoons elderflower cordial instead of orange flower water. Bake as above. Thinly slice 100 g (3½ oz) gooseberries. Heat in a saucepan with 2 tablespoons water for 2 minutes, until soft. Melt 2 tablespoons gooseberry jam and press through a sieve. Mix with 1 tablespoon boiling water and the gooseberries. Whip 150 ml (¼ pint) double cream with 3 tablespoons elderflower cordial and spread over the cooled cakes. Spoon the gooseberry mixture on top.

honey & banana cakes

Makes **12**

Preparation time **20 minutes**, plus cooling

Cooking time **25 minutes**

125 g (4 oz) **plain flour**

1 teaspoon **baking powder**

¼ teaspoon **bicarbonate of soda**

75 g (3 oz) **lightly salted butter**, melted

75 g (3 oz) **light muscovado sugar**

2 **eggs**, beaten

2 small, **very ripe bananas**, mashed

Frosting

100 g (3½ oz) **unsalted butter**, softened

5 tablespoons **clear honey**

5 tablespoons **icing sugar**

dried banana slices (optional)

Line a 12-section bun tray with paper cake cases. Sift the flour, baking powder and bicarbonate of soda into a bowl.

Mix together the melted butter, muscovado sugar, eggs and mashed bananas in a separate bowl. Tip in the dry ingredients and mix together gently until evenly combined. Divide the cake mixture between the paper cases.

Bake in a preheated oven, 160°C (325°F), Gas Mark 3, for 25 minutes or until risen and just firm to the touch. Transfer to a wire rack to cool.

Beat together the butter, honey and icing sugar in a bowl until smooth and creamy. Spread over the tops of the cakes using a small palette knife. Decorate with dried banana slices, if liked.

For yogurt & banana cakes, mash 1 large, very ripe banana. Beat together 100 g (3½ oz) softened lightly salted butter and 75 g (3 oz) light muscovado sugar until pale and creamy. Beat in the banana, 1 egg and 150 g (5 oz) Greek yogurt. Sift 150 g (5 oz) self-raising flour and ½ teaspoon baking powder into the bowl and stir in gently. Divide between 12 paper cake cases and bake as above. Transfer to a wire rack and drizzle each cake with 1 teaspoon maple syrup. Serve warm or cold.

rhubarb crumble cupcakes

Makes **12**

Preparation time **20 minutes**, plus cooling

Cooking time **45 minutes– 1 hour**

sunflower oil, for brushing

275 g (9 oz) **young rhubarb**, trimmed and cut into 1 cm (½ inch) lengths

200 g (7 oz) **light muscovado sugar**

175 g (6 oz) **lightly salted butter**, softened

225 g (7½ oz) **self-raising flour**

1 teaspoon **baking powder**

½ teaspoon **ground cinnamon**

3 **eggs**

3 tablespoons **flaked almonds**

icing sugar, for dusting

Line a 12-section muffin tray with paper muffin cases. Lightly brush a foil-lined baking sheet with oil and scatter with the rhubarb. Sprinkle with 25 g (1 oz) of the muscovado sugar and bake in a preheated oven, 200°C (400°F), Gas Mark 6, for 20–30 minutes or until tender and beginning to darken around the edges. Leave to cool. Reduce the oven to 180°C (350°F), Gas Mark 4.

Put a further 150 g (5 oz) of the sugar, 150 g (5 oz) of the butter, 175 g (6 oz) of the flour, the baking powder, cinnamon and eggs in a bowl and beat with a hand-held electric whisk for about a minute until light and creamy. Divide the cake mixture between the paper cases, spreading it fairly level, and top with the rhubarb pieces.

Put the remaining butter and flour in a food processor and process until the mixture resembles coarse breadcrumbs. Add the remaining muscovado sugar and process briefly until mixed. Scatter over the cakes and sprinkle with the almonds.

Bake for 25–30 minutes, until risen and golden. Transfer to a wire rack to cool. Serve dusted with icing sugar.

For raspberry oat crumble cupcakes, make the cake mixture as above, but replace 25 g (1 oz) of the flour with 25 g (1 oz) porridge oats. Divide between the paper cases and level the tops. Spoon 1 teaspoon raspberry jam into each case. Put 25 g (1 oz) plain flour, 25 g (1 oz) porridge oats and 25 g (1 oz) butter in a food processor and process until the mixture starts to bind together. Add 25 g (1 oz) demerara sugar and process briefly until combined. Scatter into the cases, sprinkle with the flaked almonds and bake as above.

passionfruit cream cupcakes

Makes **12**

Preparation time **20 minutes**, plus cooling

Cooking time **20–25 minutes**

150 g (5 oz) **lightly salted butter**, softened

150 g (5 oz) **caster sugar**

3 **eggs**

150 g (5 oz) **self-raising flour**

½ teaspoon **baking powder**

1 teaspoon **vanilla extract**

4 **passionfruit**

150 ml (¼ pint) **double cream**

100–150 g (3½–5 oz) **icing sugar**, plus 1 tablespoon

Line a 12-section muffin tray with paper muffin cases. Put the butter, caster sugar, eggs, flour, baking powder and vanilla extract in a bowl and beat with a hand-held electric whisk for about a minute until light and creamy. Divide the mixture between the paper cases.

Bake in a preheated oven, 180°C (350°F), Gas Mark 4, for 20–25 minutes or until risen and just firm to the touch. Transfer to a wire rack to cool.

Halve 2 of the passionfruit and scoop the pulp into a bowl with the cream and 1 tablespoon of the icing sugar. Whip until the cream only just holds its shape.

Peel away the cases from the cakes and split each cake in half horizontally. Sandwich together with the passionfruit cream.

Scoop the pulp of the remaining 2 passionfruit into a bowl. Gradually beat in the remaining icing sugar until you have a thin icing and spread over the cakes.

For peach & redcurrant cupcakes, make and bake the cakes as above. Leave to cool and split horizontally. Whip 150 ml (¼ pint) double cream with 1 tablespoon orange-flavoured liqueur or orange juice and spoon over the bottom halves of the cakes. Pile 1 thinly sliced stoned ripe peach and 75 g (3 oz) redcurrants on top, then add the lids. Dust generously with icing sugar.

mile-high marshmallow cupcakes

Makes **12**
Preparation time **25 minutes**,
  plus cooling
Cooking time **25 minutes**

50 g (2 oz) **marshmallows**
125 g (4 oz) **lightly salted
  butter**, softened
100 g (3½ oz) **caster sugar**
2 **eggs**
150 g (5 oz) **self-raising flour**
½ teaspoon **baking powder**
1 teaspoon **vanilla extract**

Topping
75 g (3 oz) **marshmallows**,
  plus extra chopped pieces
  to scatter
300 ml (½ pint) **double
  cream**

Line a 12-section bun tray with paper cake cases. Cut the marshmallows into pieces using kitchen scissors.

Put all the remaining cake ingredients in a bowl and beat with a hand-held electric whisk for about a minute until light and creamy. Stir in the marshmallow pieces and then divide the cake mixture between the paper cases.

Bake in a preheated oven, 180°C (350°F), Gas Mark 4, for 20 minutes or until risen and just firm to the touch. Transfer to a wire rack to cool.

Cut the marshmallows for the topping into small pieces and put about a third in a small saucepan with half the cream. Heat very gently until melted. Tip into a bowl and leave to cool.

Whip the remaining cream in a bowl until just holding its shape. Stir in the marshmallow cream and remaining marshmallow pieces, then pile on to the cakes. Scatter with extra chopped marshmallow pieces to serve.

For pink coconut cupcakes, grate 100 g (3½ oz) pink and white coconut ice. Make the cake mixture as above, but add the grated coconut to the bowl with the other cake ingredients, use 50 g (2 oz) caster sugar rather than 100 g (3½ oz) and omit the marshmallows. Bake as above. Whip 200 ml (7 fl oz) double cream with 1 tablespoon icing sugar until just peaking. Pile on to the cooled cakes and scatter with extra grated coconut ice.

plum polenta cupcakes

Makes **9**
Preparation time **20 minutes**
Cooking time **20–25 minutes**

mild olive oil or **vegetable oil**, for brushing
150 g (5 oz) **polenta**
100 g (3½ oz) **caster sugar**
1 teaspoon **baking powder**
75 g (3 oz) **ground almonds**
½ teaspoon **almond extract**
75 ml (3 fl oz) **soured cream**
3 tablespoons **mild olive oil** or **vegetable oil**
finely grated **rind** of 1 **lemon**, plus 4 teaspoons **juice**
2 **eggs**
2 **fresh red plums**, stoned and cut into thin wedges
2 tablespoons **clear honey**

Brush 9 sections of a 12-section muffin tray, preferably non-stick, lightly with oil. Mix together the polenta, sugar, baking powder and ground almonds in a bowl.

Whisk together the almond extract, soured cream, oil, lemon rind and eggs in a separate bowl until combined. Add to the dry ingredients and mix to a thick paste.

Divide the cake mixture between the tin sections and arrange a couple of plum wedges on top of each.

Bake in a preheated oven, 180°C (350°F), Gas Mark 4, for 20–25 minutes or until risen and beginning to colour around the edges.

Leave in the tin for 5 minutes, then loosen the edges with a knife and transfer to a wire rack.

Pierce the tops of the cakes with a skewer. Mix together the lemon juice and honey and drizzle over the cakes while still warm.

For pineapple & coconut cupcakes, put 100 g (3½ oz) caster sugar in a food processor with 75 g (3 oz) desiccated coconut and process until well blended. Mix with the polenta and baking powder as above (omit the ground almonds). Continue to make the cake mixture as above, but use the finely grated rind of 1 lime instead of the lemon. Divide the cake mixture between all 12 sections of the muffin tray and top with thin slices of peeled and cored fresh pineapple instead of the plums before baking as above. Pierce the tops of the cooked cakes with a skewer. Mix 4 teaspoons lime juice with 2 tablespoons clear honey and drizzle over the warm cakes.

malty raisin cupcakes

Makes **12**
Preparation time **10 minutes**,
  plus standing
Cooking time **20 minutes**

40 g (1½ oz) **lightly salted
  butter**, cut into pieces
75 g (3 oz) **bran flakes**
225 ml (8 fl oz) **milk**
100 g (3½ oz) **agave nectar**
  or **light muscovado sugar**
125 g (4 oz) **raisins**
125 g (4 oz) **self-raising flour**
½ teaspoon **baking powder**

Line a 12-section bun tray with paper cake cases. Put the butter and bran flakes in a heatproof bowl.

Bring the milk almost to the boil in a saucepan and pour into the bowl. Leave to stand for 10−15 minutes until the bran flakes are very soft and the mixture has cooled slightly, then stir in the agave nectar or sugar and raisins.

Sift the flour and baking powder into the bowl and then stir until just mixed. Divide the cake mixture between the paper cases.

Bake in a preheated oven, 180°C (350°F), Gas Mark 4, for 20 minutes or until slightly risen and just firm to the touch. Transfer to a wire rack to cool.

For creamy cinnamon butter, to serve with the cakes, beat 100 g (3½ oz) softened lightly salted butter in a bowl with 50 g (2 oz) golden icing sugar until light and fluffy. Mix ½ teaspoon ground cinnamon with 2 teaspoons boiling water and add to butter mixture. Beat until evenly combined. Turn into a small bowl and serve with the cupcakes, either piling the butter on top or using to split and fill the cakes.

poppy seed & lemon cupcakes

Makes **12**

Preparation time **20 minutes**, plus cooling

Cooking time **about 1 hour**

2 **unwaxed lemons**

100 g (3½ oz) **ground hazelnuts**

50 g (2 oz) **spelt flour**

1 teaspoon **baking powder**

2 tablespoons **poppy seeds**

3 **eggs**

5 tablespoons **agave nectar** plus extra to drizzle

50 g (2 oz) **lightly salted butter**, melted

50 g (2 oz) **sultanas**

Line a 12-section bun tray with paper cake cases. Cut one lemon into 12 thin slices. Put with the whole lemon in a small saucepan and cover with boiling water. Simmer very gently for 20–30 minutes until the slices are tender. Drain the slices and reserve. Cook the whole lemon for a further 15 minutes until soft and squashy. Drain and leave to cool.

Halve the whole lemon and discard the pips. Roughly chop, put in a food processor and process to a purée.

Mix the ground hazelnuts in a bowl with the flour, baking powder and poppy seeds. Mix the eggs with the lemon purée, agave nectar or sugar and melted butter and add to the dry ingredients with the sultanas. Stir until evenly combined.

Divide the cake mixture between the paper cases and place a reserved lemon slice on top. Drizzle each lemon slice with a little extra agave nectar.

Bake in a preheated oven, 180°C (350°F), Gas Mark 4, for 20 minutes or until risen and lightly browned. Transfer to a wire rack to cool.

For Brazil nut & orange cupcakes, cook 1 small orange as above. Drain, put in a food processor with the eggs, melted butter, agave nectar and sultanas and process to a purée. Chop and then grind 100 g (3½ oz) Brazil nuts. Mix with the flour and baking powder as above, adding ½ teaspoon ground allspice (omit the poppy seeds). Combine with the orange purée mixture and bake as above, with a whole Brazil nut on top of each cake.

iced gingerbread cupcakes

Makes **18**

Preparation time **20 minutes**,
  plus cooling

Cooking time **30 minutes**

225 g (7½ oz) **plain flour**

2 teaspoons **ground ginger**

1 teaspoon **baking powder**

½ teaspoon **bicarbonate
  of soda**

75 g (3 oz) **lightly salted
  butter**, cut into pieces

100 g (3½ oz) **light
  muscovado sugar**

150 g (5 oz) **black treacle**,
  plus extra to decorate

150 ml (¼ pint) **milk**

1 **egg**, beaten

100 g (3½ oz) **mixed
  dried fruit**

150 g (5 oz) **icing sugar**

3–4 teaspoons **water**

Line 2 x 12-section bun trays with 18 paper cake cases.
Put the flour, ginger, baking powder and bicarbonate of
soda in a bowl.

Put the butter in a small saucepan with the muscovado
sugar and treacle and heat until the butter has melted
and the sugar has dissolved. Remove from the heat and
stir in the milk, then the egg. Add to the dry ingredients
with the dried fruit and mix well. Divide the cake
mixture between the paper cases.

Bake in a preheated oven, 160°C (325°F), Gas Mark 3,
for 25 minutes or until risen and just firm to the touch.
Transfer to a wire rack to cool.

Mix the icing sugar with the water to make a thick icing
and drizzle over the cakes. Drizzle thin streaks of
treacle over the icing.

For mini fruity parkins, make the cake mixture as
above, but replace 50 g (2 oz) of the flour with 50 g
(2 oz) medium oatmeal, use 50 g (2 oz) mixed dried
fruit and add 50 g (2 oz) roughly chopped stoned
dried dates or figs, or prunes. Once spooned into
the paper cases, sprinkle with extra oatmeal before
baking as above. Omit the icing.

breakfast fruit & nut cupcakes

Makes **12**
Preparation time **10 minutes**
Cooking time **15 minutes**

butter, for greasing (optional)
65 g (2½ oz) **porridge oats**
100 g (3½ oz) **pecan nuts** or
  walnuts, roughly chopped
100 g (3½ oz) **blanched**
  almonds, roughly chopped
50 g (2 oz) **flaked almonds**
50 g (2 oz) **ground almonds**
150 g (5 oz) **stoned dried**
  dates, roughly chopped
50 g (2 oz) **raisins**
75 ml (3 fl oz) **agave nectar**

Line a 12-section bun tray with paper cake cases, or lightly grease the sections. Lightly toast the porridge oats by stirring them over a gentle heat in a dry frying pan. Mix with all the remaining ingredients except the agave nectar in a bowl.

Add the agave nectar and mix well until the ingredients start to bind together – this is best done with your hands. Divide the cake mixture between the paper cases and press down gently.

Bake in a preheated oven, 200°C (400°F), Gas Mark 6, for 15 minutes. Transfer to a wire rack to cool.

For spiced apricot & hazelnut cupcakes, make the cake mixture as above, but use 100 g (3½ oz) hazelnuts and 150 g (5 oz) chopped plump ready-to-eat dried apricots in place of the pecan nuts or walnuts and dates and add ½ teaspoon ground mixed spice and ½ teaspoon ground cinnamon. Bake as above.

chocolate cupcakes

chocolate fudge cupcakes

Makes **12**
Preparation time **20 minutes**
Cooking time **25 minutes**

125 g (4 oz) **lightly salted butter**, softened
150 g (5 oz) **light muscovado sugar**
2 **eggs**
100 g (3½ oz) **self-raising flour**
50 g (2 oz) **cocoa powder**
½ teaspoon **baking powder**
1 quantity **Chocolate Fudge Frosting** (see page 18)

Line a 12-section bun tray with paper cake cases. Put the butter, muscovado sugar, eggs, flour, cocoa powder and baking powder in a bowl and beat with a hand-held electric whisk for about a minute until light and creamy. Divide the cake mixture evenly between the paper cases.

Bake in a preheated oven, 180°C (350°F), Gas Mark 4, for 20 minutes or until risen and just firm to the touch. Transfer to a wire rack.

Spread the frosting over the tops of the cakes while still warm.

For white chocolate fudge cakes, make and bake the cakes as above. Make 1 quantity of White Chocolate Fudge Frosting (see page 18) instead of the Chocolate Fudge Frosting and swirl over the tops of the cakes while still warm.

chocolate crunchies

Makes **10**
Preparation time **10 minutes**,
  plus setting

150 g (5 oz) **all-butter
  shortbread biscuits**
50 g (2 oz) **white chocolate,**
  chopped
50 g (2 oz) **milk chocolate,**
  chopped
250 g (8 oz) **plain chocolate,**
  chopped
2 tablespoons **milk**
75 g (3 oz) **lightly salted
  butter**
1 tablespoon **golden syrup**
chocolate curls, to decorate
  (optional)

Line 10 sections of a 12-section bun tray with paper cake cases. Put the biscuits in a polythene bag and bash with a rolling pin to break up.

Mix the biscuit pieces with the white and milk chocolate in a bowl.

Put the plain chocolate in a heatproof bowl with the milk, butter and golden syrup. Set the bowl over a saucepan of very gently simmering water and leave until the chocolate and butter have melted, stirring frequently until smooth. Leave until cool but not beginning to set.

Tip in the biscuits and chopped chocolate and mix until coated in the melted chocolate mixture. Divide the mixture between the paper cases and leave to set. If liked, decorate with chocolate curls and put in ramekins before serving.

For chocolate fruit & nut cupcakes, melt the plain chocolate with the milk, butter and golden syrup as above, then scatter over 40 g (1½ oz) finely chopped stem ginger. Leave to cool but not beginning to set. Sprinkle in 100 g (3½ oz) chopped walnuts, 75 g (3 oz) chopped stoned dried dates and 50 g (2 oz) raisins. Stir gently to mix, then divide the mixture between the paper cases and leave to set.

chocolate cheesecakes

Makes **6**

Preparation time **25 minutes**, plus cooling

Cooking time **25 minutes**

100 g (3½ oz) **digestive biscuits**

1 teaspoon **ground ginger**

40 g (1½ oz) **lightly salted butter**, melted

200 g (7 oz) **light cream cheese**

75 g (3 oz) **light muscovado sugar**

1 **egg**

100 g (3½ oz) **plain chocolate**, chopped

2 tablespoons **brandy** or **orange-flavoured liqueur**

1 tablespoon **water**

150 ml (¼ pint) **double cream**

chocolate curls or **chocolate shards**, to decorate

Put the biscuits in a polythene bag and crush with a rolling pin or process in a food processor until crushed. Mix with the ginger and melted butter.

Divide the biscuit mixture between 6 double-thickness paper muffin cases and press down firmly with the back of a teaspoon. Place in the sections of a muffin tray.

Beat the cream cheese in a bowl with the sugar and egg. Put the chocolate with the brandy or liqueur and water in a heatproof bowl, set over a saucepan of very gently simmering water and leave until melted, stirring frequently until smooth. Stir into the cream cheese mixture and divide between the paper cases.

Bake in a preheated oven, 160°C (325°F), Gas Mark 3, for 20 minutes or until the surface feels lightly set – the cheesecakes will set further as they cool. Leave in the tin to cool completely.

Whip the cream in a bowl until just holding its shape. Remove the cheesecakes from the paper cases and top with a spoonful of cream. Decorate with chocolate curls or shards.

For chocolate honeycomb cheesecakes, make the biscuit base as above, but omit the ginger. Divide between the paper cases. Make the cheesecake mixture as above, but reduce the sugar to 50 g (2 oz) and use 100 g (3½ oz) chopped white chocolate instead of the plain chocolate. Once cool, spread with a little whipped cream and scatter with 75 g (3 oz) roughly crushed chocolate-covered honeycomb sweets.

white chocolate curl cakes

Makes **18**

Preparation time **25 minutes**, plus cooling

Cooking time **25 minutes**

150 g (5 oz) **lightly salted butter**, softened

150 g (5 oz) **caster sugar**

175 g (6 oz) **self-raising flour**

3 **eggs**

1 teaspoon **vanilla extract**

50 g (2 oz) **white chocolate chips**

100 g (3½ oz) chunky piece of **white chocolate**

1 quantity **White Chocolate Fudge Frosting** (see page 18)

icing sugar, for dusting

Line 2 x 12-section bun tray with 18 paper cake cases. Put the butter, caster sugar, flour, eggs and vanilla extract in a bowl and beat with a hand-held electric whisk for 1–2 minutes until light and creamy. Stir in the chocolate chips. Divide the cake mixture evenly between the paper cases.

Bake in a preheated oven, 180°C (350°F), Gas Mark 4, for 20 minutes or until risen and just firm to the touch. Transfer to a wire rack to cool.

Pare curls from the piece of chocolate using a vegetable peeler – if the chocolate breaks off in small, brittle shards, try softening it in a microwave oven for a few seconds first, but take care not to overheat and melt it. Set the chocolate curls aside in a cool place while icing the cakes.

Spread the chocolate frosting all over the tops of the cakes using a small palette knife. Pile the chocolate curls on to the cakes and lightly dust with icing sugar.

For chocolate coconut kisses, make and bake the cakes as above. Leave to cool. Melt 175 g (6 oz) white chocolate (see pages 16–17). Transfer a third of the melted chocolate to a small bowl and stir 75 g (3 oz) shredded coconut into the remaining larger quantity of melted chocolate. Spread a thin layer of melted chocolate over the tops of the cakes and pile the coconut mixture on top. Leave to set.

chocolate orange cupcakes

Makes **12**

Preparation time **20 minutes**,
  plus cooling

Cooking time **25 minutes**

125 g (4 oz) **lightly salted
  butter**, softened
125 g (4 oz) **caster sugar**
2 **eggs**
125 g (4 oz) **self-raising flour**
25 g (1 oz) **cocoa powder**
½ teaspoon **baking powder**
finely grated **rind** of 1 **orange**
**candied orange peel
  shavings**, to decorate
  (optional)

Icing
100 g (3½ oz) **plain
  chocolate**, chopped
100 g (3½ oz) **unsalted
  butter**, softened
125 g (4 oz) **icing sugar**
2 tablespoons **cocoa powder**

Line a 12-section bun tray with paper cake cases.
Put the lightly salted butter, caster sugar, eggs, flour,
cocoa powder, baking powder and orange rind in a
bowl and beat with a hand-held electric whisk for about
a minute until light and creamy. Divide the cake mixture
evenly between the paper cases.

Bake in a preheated oven, 180°C (350°F), Gas Mark 4,
for 20 minutes or until risen and just firm to the touch.
Transfer to a wire rack to cool.

Melt the chocolate (see pages 16–17) and leave to
cool. Beat together the unsalted butter, icing sugar and
cocoa powder in a bowl until smooth and creamy. Stir in
the melted chocolate. Pipe or swirl the icing over the
tops of the cakes and decorate with candied orange
peel shavings, if liked.

For chocolate prune cupcakes, chop 75 g (3 oz)
stoned prunes into small pieces and put in a small
bowl with 2 teaspoons brandy. Leave to soak for
30 minutes. Make the cake mixture as above, stirring
in any unabsorbed brandy from the prunes, and divide
between the paper cases. Arrange the prunes on top
and bake as above. Once cooled, scribble with 25 g
(1 oz) melted plain chocolate.

chocolate peanut cupcakes

Makes **12**
Preparation time **25 minutes**,
  plus cooling & setting
Cooking time **30 minutes**

150 g (5 oz) **lightly salted
  butter**, softened
250 g (8 oz) **caster sugar**
3 **eggs**
150 g (5 oz) **self-raising flour**
25 g (1 oz) **cocoa powder**
½ teaspoon **baking powder**
50 g (2 oz) **salted peanuts**
3 tablespoons **water**
75 ml (3 fl oz) **double cream**
25 g (1 oz) **unsalted butter**
100 g (3½ oz) **plain
  chocolate**, chopped
1 tablespoon **golden syrup**

Line a 12-section muffin tray with paper muffin cases. Put the lightly salted butter, 150 g (5 oz) of the sugar, the eggs, flour, cocoa powder and baking powder in a bowl and beat with a hand-held electric whisk for about a minute until light and creamy. Divide the cake mixture between the paper cases.

Bake in a preheated oven, 180°C (350°F), Gas Mark 4, for 20 minutes or until risen and just firm to the touch. Transfer to a wire rack to cool.

Chop the peanuts finely. Put the remaining sugar in a small saucepan with the water and heat gently until the sugar has dissolved. Bring to the boil and boil rapidly for 4–5 minutes until the syrup has turned pale golden. Dip the base of the pan in cold water to prevent further cooking.

Add 50 ml (2 fl oz) of the cream and the unsalted butter to the syrup and heat very gently, stirring, to make a smooth caramel. Stir in the chopped nuts and leave until cool but not set. Spoon over the cupcakes.

Melt the chocolate with the remaining cream and golden syrup in a small saucepan over a gentle heat. Spoon over the cakes and leave to set.

For chocolate jaffa cupcakes, make the cake mixture as above, but add the finely grated rind of ½ orange. Bake as above and leave to cool. Heat 5 tablespoons orange jelly marmalade in a small saucepan with 1 teaspoon water until melted. Leave until cool but not set. Spread over the tops of the cakes. Melt 100 g (3½ oz) plain chocolate (see pages 16–17) and spoon over the cakes. Leave to set.

triple chocolate cupcakes

Makes **12**

Preparation time **30 minutes**,
  plus cooling & setting

Cooking time **25 minutes**

100 g (3½ oz) **white
  chocolate**, chopped
100 g (3½ oz) **milk
  chocolate**, chopped
100 g (3½ oz) **plain
  chocolate**, chopped
40 g (1½ oz) **unsalted butter**
12 **Chocolate Cupcakes**
  (see page 22)
cocoa powder, for dusting

Put the white, milk and plain chocolate in separate microwave-proof or heatproof bowls and add a third of the butter to each. Melt all the chocolate, either one at a time in a microwave oven or by setting each bowl over a saucepan of very gently simmering water, stirring occasionally until smooth.

Spread the melted white chocolate over 4 of the cakes using a small palette knife and dust with a little cocoa powder.

Put 2 tablespoons of the melted milk and plain chocolate in separate piping bags fitted with writing nozzles. Spread the milk chocolate over 4 more of the cakes and pipe dots of plain chocolate over the milk chocolate.

Spread the plain chocolate over the 4 remaining cakes and scribble with lines of piped milk chocolate. Leave to set.

For double chocolate whirls, make and bake the cake mixture as on page 22, but scatter 75 g (3 oz) chopped milk chocolate over the mixture in the cases before baking. Once baked, leave to cool. Whip 200 ml (7 fl oz) double cream with 1 tablespoon icing sugar until only just beginning to hold its shape. Put in a piping bag fitted with a large star nozzle and pipe swirls on the tops of the cakes, leaving a dip in the centre. Melt 75 g (3 oz) plain chocolate with 15 g (½ oz) butter and 1 tablespoon golden syrup and spoon into the centres.

minted white chocolate cakes

Makes **12**
Preparation time **20 minutes**
Cooking time **20 minutes**

8 g (¼ oz) **mint leaves**
100 g (3½ oz) **caster sugar**
125 g (4 oz) **lightly salted butter**, softened
2 **eggs**
150 g (5 oz) **self-raising flour**
½ teaspoon **baking powder**
175 g (6 oz) **white chocolate**, chopped
icing sugar, for dusting

Line a 12-section bun tray with paper cake cases. Put the mint leaves in a heatproof bowl, cover with boiling water and leave for 30 seconds. Drain and pat dry on kitchen paper. Put the leaves in a food processor with the caster sugar and process until the mint is finely chopped.

Transfer the mint sugar to a bowl and add the butter, eggs, flour and baking powder. Beat with a hand-held electric whisk for about a minute until light and creamy.

Stir in 100 g (3½ oz) of the chocolate and then divide the cake mixture between the paper cases. Scatter with the remaining chocolate.

Bake in a preheated oven, 180°C (350°F), Gas Mark 4, for 20 minutes or until the cakes are risen and just firm to the touch. Transfer to a wire rack to cool. Lightly dust with icing sugar.

For white-chocolate-frosted cardamom cakes, make the cake mixture as above, but omit the mint, simply including the sugar with the other cake ingredients before beating, and add the crushed seeds of 10 cardamom pods. Bake as above and leave to cool. Heat 150 ml (¼ pint) double cream in a small saucepan until it bubbles up around the edge. Remove from the heat and stir in 150 g (5 oz) chopped white chocolate. Stir until melted, then turn into a bowl and leave to cool. Once cool enough to hold its shape when stirred, spoon on to the tops of the cakes and swirl with the back of the spoon.

chocolate strawberry cupcakes

Makes **12**
Preparation time **30 minutes**,
  plus cooling
Cooking time **30 minutes**

75 g (3 oz) **cocoa powder**
225 ml (7½ fl oz) **boiling
  water**
125 g (4 oz) **lightly salted
  butter**, softened
275 g (9 oz) **light
  muscovado sugar**
2 **eggs**
200 g (7 oz) **plain flour**
1 teaspoon **baking powder**
whipped cream, to serve
  (optional)

To decorate
150 ml (¼ pint) **double
  cream**
4 tablespoons **icing sugar**
4 tablespoons **water**
275 g (9 oz) **plain chocolate**,
  chopped
12 **fresh strawberries**

Line a 12-section muffin tray with paper muffin cases. Put the cocoa powder in a heatproof bowl and whisk in the boiling water. Leave to cool.

Beat together the butter and muscovado sugar in a separate bowl until pale and creamy. Gradually beat in the eggs. Sift the flour into the bowl and stir in, then add the cocoa mixture and stir in. Divide the cake mixture between the paper cases.

Bake in a preheated oven, 180°C (350°F), Gas Mark 4, for 25 minutes or until risen and just firm. Leave to cool in the tin for 10 minutes, then transfer to a wire rack to cool completely.

Put the cream, icing sugar and water in a small saucepan and bring just to the boil. Remove from the heat and stir in 200 g (7 oz) of the chocolate. Leave to cool, stirring frequently until smooth and glossy.

Peel away the paper cases and spoon a little of the chocolate mixture over each cake, swirling it slightly down the sides using a small palette knife.

Melt the remaining chocolate (see pages 16–17). Half dip the strawberries in the chocolate and position on the cakes. Serve with whipped cream, if liked.

For chocolate almond sandwich cakes, make the cake mixture as above, divide between the cases and scatter with 3 tablespoons flaked almonds. Bake as above and leave to cool. Whip 150 ml (¼ pint) double cream with 1 tablespoon icing sugar and 1 tablespoon almond-flavoured liqueur. Halve the cakes horizontally and sandwich with the cream. Dust with icing sugar.

warm chocolate brownie cakes

Makes **about 18**
Preparation time **10 minutes**
Cooking time **12 minutes**

100 g (3½ oz) **milk chocolate**
100 g (3½ oz) **pecan nuts** or
  walnuts
200 g (7 oz) **plain chocolate**,
  chopped
150 g (5 oz) **lightly salted
  butter**
3 **eggs**
200 g (7 oz) **light
  muscovado sugar**
125 g (4 oz) **self-raising flour**
½ teaspoon **baking powder**
cocoa powder, for dusting
ice cream, to serve

Line a 12-section bun tray with paper cake cases.
Chop the milk chocolate and nuts into small pieces.

Melt the plain chocolate with the butter (see pages
16–17), stirring frequently until smooth.

Beat together the eggs and sugar in a bowl, then stir
in the melted chocolate and butter. Sift the flour and
baking powder into the bowl and stir in gently.

Stir in the milk chocolate and nuts and then divide the
cake mixture between the paper cases.

Bake in a preheated oven, 190°C (375°F), Gas Mark 5,
for 12 minutes or until a crust has formed but the cakes
feel quite soft underneath. Leave to cool in the tin for
10 minutes.

Transfer to plates and top with small scoops of ice
cream and a dusting of cocoa powder, if liked.
Alternatively, serve cold.

For chocolate blondie cupcakes, chop 200 g (7 oz)
white chocolate into small pieces. Melt a further 100 g
(3½ oz) chopped white chocolate with 75 g (3 oz)
butter in a small bowl. Beat together 3 eggs and
100 g (3½ oz) caster sugar in a separate bowl.
Stir in the melted chocolate mixture. Sift 125 g (4 oz)
self-raising flour into the bowl and stir in gently with
100 g (3½ oz) chopped blanched almonds and the
chopped chocolate. Divide between the paper cases
and bake as above.

chocolate toffee cupcakes

Makes **12**

Preparation time **25 minutes**,
  plus cooling & setting

Cooking time **30 minutes**

200 g (7 oz) (about ½ can)
  **sweetened condensed
  milk**
50 g (2 oz) **caster sugar**
65 g (2½ oz) **unsalted butter**
2 tablespoons **golden syrup**
12 **Vanilla Cupcakes**
  (see page 22)
100 g (3½ oz) **plain
  chocolate**, chopped
100 g (3½ oz) **milk
  chocolate**, chopped

Put the condensed milk, sugar, butter and golden syrup in a medium, heavy-based saucepan and heat gently, stirring, until the sugar has dissolved. Cook over a gentle heat, stirring, for 5 minutes or until the mixture has turned a pale fudge colour.

Leave to cool for 2 minutes, then spoon the toffee over the top of the cooled cakes.

Melt the plain and milk chocolate separately (see pages 16–17). Place a couple of teaspoons of each type of melted chocolate on to a cake and tap the cake on the work surface to level the chocolate. Swirl the chocolates together using the tip of a cocktail stick or fine skewer to marble them lightly.

Repeat on the remaining cakes. Leave the chocolate to set before serving.

For mint chocolate cupcakes, mix 200 g (7 oz) icing sugar with 1 teaspoon natural mint extract and 1–2 teaspoons water in a bowl so that the icing is smooth and just holds its shape. Spread over the tops of the cooled cooked cakes with a palette knife and leave until lightly set. Melt 100 g (3½ oz) plain chocolate and spread over the tops of the cakes.

rich fruit chocolate cupcakes

Makes **8**
Preparation time **15 minutes**
Cooking time **35 minutes**

65 g (2½ oz) **lightly salted butter**, softened
65 g (2½ oz) **light muscovado sugar**
65 g (2½ oz) **plain flour**
15 g (½ oz) **cocoa powder**
1 teaspoon **ground mixed spice**
1 **egg**
50 g (2 oz) **chopped mixed nuts**
100 g (3½ oz) **milk chocolate**, chopped
25 g (1 oz) **glacé ginger**, chopped
100 g (3½ oz) **mixed dried fruit**
demerara sugar, for sprinkling

Line 8 sections of a 12-section bun tray with paper cake cases. Beat together the butter and muscovado sugar with a hand-held electric whisk until pale and creamy. Sift together the flour, cocoa powder and mixed spice.

Gradually beat the egg into the butter and sugar mixture, then stir in the flour mixture.

Reserve 2 tablespoons each of the nuts and chocolate and stir the remainder into the cake mixture with the ginger and fruit. Mix well.

Divide the cake mixture between the paper cases. Scatter with the reserved nuts and chocolate and sprinkle with a little demerara sugar.

Bake in a preheated oven, 150°C (300°F), Gas Mark 2, for 35 minutes or until firm to the touch. Transfer to a wire rack to cool and wrap in extra, decorative paper case, if liked.

For apricot & white chocolate cupcakes, make the cake mixture as above, but use an extra 15 g (½ oz) plain flour instead of the cocoa powder and 1 teaspoon vanilla extract in place of the mixed spice. Replace the mixed nuts with 50 g (2 oz) finely chopped blanched almonds and the milk chocolate with 100 g (3½ oz) chopped white chocolate, reserve 2 tablespoons each and add the remainder to the mixture with 100 g (3½ oz) finely chopped ready-to-eat dried apricots instead of the mixed dried fruit (omit the ginger). Spoon the cake mixture into the paper cases with the reserved almonds and white chocolate, sprinkle with a little demerara sugar and bake as above.

mocha cupcakes

Makes **12**

Preparation time **15 minutes**, plus cooling & setting

Cooking time **30 minutes**

250 ml (8 fl oz) **water**

250 g (8 oz) **caster sugar**

125 g (4 oz) **lightly salted butter**

2 tablespoons **cocoa powder**, sifted

½ teaspoon **bicarbonate of soda**

2 tablespoons **coffee granules**

225 g (7½ oz) **self-raising flour**

2 **eggs**, lightly beaten

Icing

150 g (5 oz) **plain chocolate**, diced

150 g (5 oz) **unsalted butter**, diced

2 tablespoons **golden syrup**

12 **chocolate-covered coffee beans**, to decorate

Line a 12-hole muffin tray with paper or foil muffin cases. Put the water and sugar in a saucepan and heat gently, stirring, until the sugar has dissolved. Stir in the lightly salted butter, cocoa powder, bicarbonate of soda and coffee granules and bring to the boil. Reduce the heat and simmer for 5 minutes, then remove from the heat and leave to cool.

Beat the flour and eggs into the cooled chocolate mixture until smooth. Divide the cake mixture between the paper or foil cases.

Bake in a preheated oven, 180°C (350°F), Gas Mark 4, for 20 minutes or until risen and firm. Transfer to a wire rack to cool.

Put the chocolate, unsalted butter and golden syrup in a heatproof bowl. Set over a saucepan of very gently simmering water and leave until the chocolate and butter have melted, stirring frequently. Leave to cool to room temperature, then chill until thickened.

Spread the icing over the tops of the cakes, decorate each with a chocolate-covered coffee bean and leave to set.

For chocolate, rum & raisin cupcakes, soak 50 g (2 oz) raisins in 2 tablespoons rum for about 1 hour until plumped up. Make the cake mixture as above, but omit the coffee granules and add the soaked raisins and any unabsorbed rum with the eggs. Bake and then ice and decorate as above.

chocolate raspberry friands

Makes **10**
Preparation time **20 minutes**
Cooking time **20 minutes**

100 g (3½ oz) **lightly salted butter**
75 g (3 oz) **plain chocolate**, at room temperature
100 g (3½ oz) **ground almonds**
125 g (4 oz) **golden caster sugar**
40 g (1½ oz) **plain flour**
3 **egg whites**
150 g (5 oz) **fresh raspberries**
icing sugar, for dusting (optional)

Line 10 sections of a 12-section bun tray with paper cake cases. Melt the butter in a small saucepan and leave to cool. Coarsely grate the chocolate – if the chocolate is brittle and difficult to grate, try softening it in a microwave oven for a few seconds first, but take care not to overheat and melt it.

Mix together the ground almonds, 75 g (3 oz) of the caster sugar and the flour in a large bowl. Stir in the melted butter and grated chocolate until just combined.

Whisk the egg whites in a thoroughly clean bowl until peaking. Gradually whisk in the remaining caster sugar. Using a large metal spoon, fold half the egg whites into the chocolate mixture to lighten it, then fold in the remainder until evenly combined.

Divide the cake mixture between the paper cases and scatter the raspberries on top.

Bake in a preheated oven, 200°C (400°F), Gas Mark 6, for 15 minutes or until golden and just firm to the touch. Transfer to a wire rack to cool. Serve dusted with icing sugar.

For white chocolate blueberry friends, make the cake mixture as above, but use 75 g (3 oz) white chocolate instead of the plain chocolate. Divide between the paper cases and scatter with 100 g (3½ oz) fresh blueberries. Bake as above and leave to cool. Scatter the cakes with a further 75 g (3 oz) blueberries and drizzle with 50 g (2 oz) melted white chocolate (see pages 16–17).

chocolate ricotta cakes

Makes **18**

Preparation time **20 minutes**, plus cooling

Cooking time **20 minutes**

150 g (5 oz) **lightly salted butter**, softened

150 g (5 oz) **golden caster sugar**

3 **eggs**

150 g (5 oz) **self-raising flour**

25 g (1 oz) **cocoa powder**, plus extra for dusting

½ teaspoon **baking powder**

Filling

250 g (8 oz) **ricotta cheese**

2 tablespoons **brandy**

75 g (3 oz) **icing sugar**

4 tablespoons **double cream**

100 g (3½ oz) **plain** or **milk chocolate**, chopped

50 g (2 oz) **flaked almonds**, chopped

50 g (2 oz) **natural glacé cherries**, chopped

Line 18 sections of 2 x 12-section bun trays with paper cake cases. Put the butter, caster sugar, eggs, flour, cocoa powder and baking powder in a bowl and beat with a hand-held electric whisk for about a minute until light and creamy. Divide the cake mixture between the paper cases.

Bake in a preheated oven, 180°C (350°F), Gas Mark 4, for 20 minutes or until risen and just firm to the touch. Transfer to a wire rack to cool.

Beat together the ricotta, brandy, icing sugar and cream in a bowl. Gently stir in the chocolate, almonds and cherries.

Cut a thick diagonal slice off the top of each cake and pile the filling on to the cut surfaces. Reposition the slices, twisting them so that the thickest part is uppermost. Serve within 24 hours, dusted with cocoa powder.

For chocolate cream butterfly cupcakes, make and bake the cupcakes as above and leave to cool. Heat 150 ml (¼ pint) double cream in a small saucepan until almost boiling. Pour into a heatproof bowl and stir in 150 g (5 oz) chopped milk or plain chocolate. Leave until the chocolate melts, stirring frequently. Once the cream is cool enough to hold its shape, put in a large piping bag fitted with a star nozzle. Use a sharp knife to cut out a round from the centre top of each cake. Cut the rounds in half. Pipe the chocolate cream into the cavities in the cakes. Reposition the 2 halves of the rounds on each cake at an angle of 45° to resemble butterfly wings. Lightly dust with icing sugar.

frosted choc 'n' nut cupcakes

Makes **12**
Preparation time **20 minutes**,
  plus cooling
Cooking time **20 minutes**

175 g (6 oz) **lightly salted
  butter**, softened
100 g (3½ oz) **caster sugar**
150 g (5 oz) **self-raising flour**
3 **eggs**
100 g (3½ oz) **ground
  almonds** or **hazelnuts**
65 g (2½ oz) **unblanched
  hazelnuts**, roughly chopped
  and toasted
75 g (3 oz) **white chocolate**,
  chopped
75 g (3 oz) **milk chocolate**,
  chopped

Frosting
250 g (8 oz) **unsalted butter**,
  softened
50 g (2 oz) **vanilla sugar**
  (see right for homemade)
100 g (3½ oz) **icing sugar**
2 teaspoons **lemon juice**

Line a 12-section muffin tray with paper muffin cases.
Put the lightly salted butter, caster sugar, flour, eggs and
ground almonds or hazelnuts in a bowl and beat with
a hand-held electric whisk for 1–2 minutes until light
and creamy.

Reserve a handful of the chopped unblanched
hazelnuts for decoration. Add the remainder to the cake
mixture with the white and milk chocolate, mix together
and then divide between the paper cases.

Bake in a preheated oven, 180°C (350°F), Gas Mark 4,
for 20 minutes or until risen and just firm to the touch.
Transfer to a wire rack to cool.

Beat together the unsalted butter, sugars and lemon
juice in a bowl until pale and fluffy. Spread the frosting
over the cakes with a small palette knife and decorate
with the reserved nuts.

For homemade vanilla sugar, tip a 500 g (1 lb) pack
of caster sugar into an airtight container. Split 2 vanilla
pods lengthways, then cut each in half. Push the
vanilla pods down into the sugar and replace the lid.
Store in a cool place for at least a week before using,
shaking the container frequently to disperse the vanilla
flavour. The sugar will keep for several months and
can be topped up with more sugar and fresh pods
when the flavour has reduced.

white chocolate maple muffins

Makes **8**
Preparation time **10 minutes**
Cooking time **20–25 minutes**

300 g (10 oz) **self-raising
flour**
1 teaspoon **baking powder**
125 g (4 oz) **soft brown
sugar**
1 **egg**
50 ml (2 fl oz) **maple syrup**
250 ml (8 fl oz) **milk**
50 g (2 oz) **lightly salted
butter**, melted
125 g (4 oz) **white chocolate**,
chopped, plus extra to
decorate
75 g (3 oz) **pecan nuts**,
roughly chopped, plus extra
to decorate

Line 8 sections of a 12-section muffin tray with paper muffin cases. Sift the flour and baking powder into a bowl and stir in the sugar.

Beat together the egg, maple syrup, milk and melted butter in a separate bowl and then mix into the dry ingredients until only just combined. Fold in the chocolate and pecan nuts.

Divide the muffin mixture between the paper cases and top with some extra chopped nuts and chocolate.

Bake in a preheated oven, 200°C (400°F), Gas Mark 6, for 20–25 minutes or until risen and golden. Transfer to a wire rack to cool.

For dark chocolate & ginger muffins, finely chop 2 pieces of stem ginger from a jar. Make the muffin mixture as above, but use 125 g (4 oz) plain chocolate instead of white chocolate, 3 tablespoons stem ginger juice in place of the maple syrup and replace 50 g (2 oz) of the flour with 50 g (2 oz) cocoa powder. Add the chopped ginger with the wet ingredients. Top with extra chopped nuts and plain chocolate and bake as above.

cupcakes
for kids

snakes in the jungle

Makes **12**

Preparation time **55 minutes**, plus cooling

Cooking time **20 minutes**

2 tablespoons **strawberry** or **raspberry jam**

12 **Vanilla Cupcakes** (see page 22)

175 g (6 oz) **green ready-to-roll icing**

icing sugar, for dusting

50 g (2 oz) **red ready-to-roll icing**

50 g (2 oz) **yellow ready-to-roll icing**

4 **flaked chocolate bars**, cut into 5 cm (2 inch) lengths

50 g (2 oz) **white ready-to-roll icing**

25 g (1 oz) **black ready-to-roll icing**

Brush the jam over the top of each cooled cake with a pastry brush. Knead the green icing on a work surface lightly dusted with icing sugar. Roll out very thinly and cut out 12 rounds using a 6 cm (2½ inch) cookie cutter. Place a green round on top of each cake.

Take a small ball of icing in any colour – about 8 g (¼ oz) – and roll under the palm of your hand into a thin sausage about 12–15 cm (5–6 inches) long, tapering it to a point at one end and shaping a head at the other. Flatten the head slightly and mark a mouth with a small, sharp knife.

Roll out a little icing in a contrasting colour thinly and cut out small diamond shapes. Secure along the snake using a dampened paintbrush. Wrap the snake around a length of flaked chocolate and position on top of a cake.

Make more snakes in the same way, kneading small amounts of the icing together to make different colours, such as red and yellow for orange or red and white for pink. For some cakes, press the chocolate vertically into the cake.

Roll small balls of white icing and press tiny balls of black icing over them for eyes. Secure to the snakes' heads with a dampened paintbrush.

For multicoloured millipedes, cover the cakes with green ready-to-roll icing as above. Arrange a snaking row of dolly mixture sweets over each, securing with dots of icing from a tube of black writing icing. Paint small dots for eyes and a smiling mouth on to the front sweet. Pipe tiny legs along the sides of the sweets.

alphabetti cupcakes

Makes **12**

Preparation time **45 minutes**, plus cooling & setting

Cooking time **20 minutes**

125 g (4 oz) **lightly salted butter**, softened

125 g (4 oz) **caster sugar**

2 **eggs**

150 g (5 oz) **self-raising flour**

½ teaspoon **baking powder**

1 teaspoon **vanilla extract**

50 g (2 oz) **white chocolate polka dots**

To decorate

100 g (3½ oz) each of **orange** and **red ready-to-roll icing** (or use other colours of your choice)

icing sugar, for dusting

50 g (2 oz) **white chocolate polka dots**, melted

Line a 12-section bun tray with paper cake cases. Put the butter, sugar, eggs, flour, baking powder and vanilla extract into a bowl and beat with a hand-held electric whisk for about a minute until light and creamy. Stir in the polka dots and then divide the cake mixture between the paper cases.

Bake in a preheated oven, 180°C (350°F), Gas Mark 4, for 20 minutes or until risen and just firm to the touch. Transfer to a wire rack to cool.

Working with one colour at a time, roll out the icing on a work surface lightly dusted with icing sugar and cut out small letter shapes using alphabet cutters. Transfer to a tray lined with baking parchment. Re-roll the trimmings to make more. Leave to set for at least 1 hour until dry and holding their shape.

Spread each cake with a thin layer of melted chocolate and scatter plenty of letters on top, if necessary securing them to one another with a dampened paintbrush.

For tumbling number cakes, make and bake the cakes as above and leave to cool. Roll out 100 g (3½ oz) each of yellow and green ready-to-roll icing on a work surface lightly dusted with icing sugar and cut out numbers using number cutters. Leave to set and decorate as above.

ladybirds

Makes **12**

Preparation time **40 minutes**, plus cooling

Cooking time **20 minutes**

2 tablespoons **raspberry** or **strawberry jam**

12 **Vanilla Cupcakes** (see page 22)

175 g (6 oz) **red ready-to-roll icing**

icing sugar, for dusting

125 g (4 oz) **black ready-to-roll icing**

15 g (½ oz) **white ready-to-roll icing**

small piece of **candied orange peel**, cut into matchstick lengths

Brush the jam over the top of each cooled cake. Knead the red icing on a work surface lightly dusted with icing sugar and roll it out. Cut out 12 rounds using a 6 cm (2½ inch) cookie cutter. Place a round on each cake.

Roll out thin strips of black icing and position one across each red round, securing with a dampened paintbrush. Roll out half the remaining black icing to a thin sausage shape, about 1 cm (½ inch) in diameter. Cut into very thin slices and secure to the cakes to represent ladybird spots.

Make oval-shaped heads from the remaining black icing and secure in position. Roll small balls of the white icing for eyes and press tiny balls of black icing over them. Secure with a dampened paintbrush.

Press the lengths of candied orange peel behind the ladybirds' heads for antennae, then press small balls of black icing on to their ends. Use tiny pieces of white icing to shape smiling mouths.

For busy bees, brush the cooled cakes with jam and use 175 g (6 oz) yellow ready-to-roll icing to cover the cakes as above instead of red icing. Use 125 g (4 oz) chocolate-flavoured ready-to-roll icing in place of black icing to shape heads and cut thin strips to lay across the cakes, securing with a dampened paintbrush. Add big eyes using a little white ready-to-roll icing. For the wings, fold small pieces of rice paper in half and cut out simple wing shapes. Make a shallow groove on top of each cake (in the same position as the black strip on the ladybirds) and gently press the fold into the groove.

frosted banana cupcakes

Makes **12**

Preparation time **25 minutes**, plus cooling

Cooking time **20 minutes**

100 g (3½ oz) **lightly salted butter**, softened

100 g (3½ oz) **golden caster sugar**

2 **eggs**

125 g (4 oz) **self-raising flour**

½ teaspoon **baking powder**

1 **ripe banana**, mashed

75 g (3 oz) **sultanas**

100 g (3½ oz) **Greek yogurt**

250 g (8 oz) **golden icing sugar**

sugar sprinkles, to decorate

Line a 12-section bun tray with paper cake cases. Put the butter, caster sugar, eggs, flour and baking powder in a bowl and beat with a hand-held electric whisk for about a minute until light and creamy. Stir in the mashed banana and sultanas. Divide the cake mixture between the paper cases.

Bake in a preheated oven, 180°C (350°F), Gas Mark 4, for 20 minutes or until risen and just firm. Transfer to a wire rack to cool.

Line a bowl with a double thickness of kitchen paper. Spoon the yogurt on to the paper. Bring up the edges and gently squeeze out as much liquid as possible. Tip the thickened ball of yogurt on to 2 more sheets of kitchen paper and squeeze out a little more liquid if possible.

Sift the icing sugar into a separate bowl and add the thick yogurt. Mix well to make an icing with a slightly fudgy texture. Swirl the mixture over the cakes and scatter with sugar sprinkles to decorate.

For clementine cupcakes, make the cake mixture as above, but omit the mashed banana and add the finely grated rind of 2 clementines. Bake as above and leave to cool. Make the thickened yogurt as above and mix with 4 tablespoons orange curd in a bowl. Swirl over the tops of the cakes and decorate with fresh clementine slices.

on the farm

Makes **12**

Preparation time **55 minutes**, plus cooling

Cooking time **20 minutes**

½ quantity **Buttercream** (see page 18)

12 **Vanilla Cupcakes** (see page 22)

100 g (3½ oz) **brown ready-to-roll icing**

icing sugar, for dusting

100 g (3½ oz) **yellow ready-to-roll icing**

100 g (3½ oz) **pink ready-to-roll icing**

15 g (½ oz) **white ready-to-roll icing**

15 g (½ oz) **black ready-to-roll icing**

black food colouring

Spread a thick layer of the buttercream over the cooled cakes. Using a palette knife, lightly peak the icing on 4 of the cakes.

Knead 75 g (3 oz) of the brown icing (wrap the remainder in clingfilm) on a work surface lightly dusted with icing sugar for the sheep. Reserve a small piece for the ears and roll the remainder into 4 balls. Flatten each ball into an oval shape and gently press on to the cakes thickly spread with buttercream. Shape and position small ears on each sheep.

Reserve a small piece of yellow icing for the ears and roll the remainder into 4 balls for the cows. Flatten into oval shapes as large as the cake tops. Gently press on to 4 more cakes. Shape and position the ears. Use the remaining brown to shape the cows' nostrils and horns, securing with a dampened paintbrush.

Reserve 25 g (1 oz) of the pink icing for the pigs' snouts and ears. Roll the remainder into 4 balls and flatten into rounds, almost as large as each cake top. Shape and position the snouts and floppy ears, pressing 2 small holes in each snout with the tip of a cocktail stick or fine skewer.

Use the white and black icing to make all the animals' eyes – their shape and size to suit each animal. Roll small balls of white icing and press tiny balls of black icing over them. Secure with a dampened paintbrush.

Use a fine paintbrush, dipped in the food colouring, to paint on additional features.

wiggly worms

Makes **11**

Preparation time **45 minutes**, plus cooling

Cooking time **20 minutes**

75 g (3 oz) **unsalted butter**, softened

125 g (4 oz) **icing sugar**, plus extra for dusting

12 **Vanilla Cupcakes** (see page 22)

50 g (2 oz) **milk chocolate**, grated

100 g (2 oz) **pink** or **red ready-to-roll icing**

50 g (3½ oz) **chocolate-flavoured ready-to-roll icing**

12 small **candy-covered chocolate sweets**

Beat together the butter and sugar in a bowl until smooth and creamy. Remove one cooled cake from its case and take a thick, angled slice off the top. Spread a little of the buttercream over another cake, position the slice on top and spread with a little more buttercream to make a larger 'face' cake.

Spread a large, rectangular board with 4 tablespoons of the buttercream and scatter with the chocolate. Spread the remaining buttercream over the cakes, then position in a snaking line over the chocolate with the face cake at the front.

Roll out the coloured icing thinly on a work surface lightly dusted with icing sugar and cut out 9 rounds using a 5 cm (2 inch) cookie cutter. Place on all the cakes except the face and end cakes. Cut out a pointed tail from the trimmings and place on the end cake. Roll out the chocolate icing and cut out a slightly larger round. Position on the front cake. Thinly roll out the chocolate icing and cut out 2.5 cm (1 inch) rounds. Place on the rest of the cakes and top each with a candy-covered chocolate sweet. Shape and position eyes and mouth using icing trimmings and the two remaining sweets.

princess cupcakes

Makes **12**

Preparation time **30 minutes**, plus cooling

Cooking time **20 minutes**

1 quantity **Buttercream** (see page 18)

a few drops of **pink food colouring**

12 **Vanilla Cupcakes** (see page 22)

edible silver balls

Divide the buttercream between 2 bowls. Add the food colouring to one bowl and mix well. Spread the pink buttercream over the tops of the cooled cakes to within 5 mm (¼ inch) of the edges using a small palette knife, doming it up slightly in the centre.

Put half the uncoloured buttercream in a piping bag fitted with a writing nozzle and the remainder in a piping bag fitted with a star nozzle. Pipe lines, 1 cm (½ inch) apart, across the pink buttercream, then across in the other direction to create a diamond pattern.

Pipe little stars around the edges using the icing in the other bag. Decorate the piped lines with silver balls.

For jewelled bangle cupcakes, make ½ quantity Buttercream (see page 18). Spread over the tops of the cooled cakes using a small palette knife. Using a tube of yellow writing icing, pipe a circle of icing 1 cm (½ inch) in from the edges of the cake. Arrange a circle of small sweets such as candy-covered chocolate drops over the circle. Top each with a dot of icing and add an edible gold or silver ball.

fruity lunchbox muffins

Makes **12**
Preparation time **10 minutes**
Cooking time **15 minutes**

100 g (3½ oz) **plain flour**
100 g (3½ oz) **wholemeal
flour**
2 teaspoons **baking powder**
75 g (3 oz) **golden
caster sugar**
2 **eggs**
2 tablespoons **mild olive oil**
or **vegetable oil**
40 g (1½ oz) **lightly salted
butter**, melted
2 teaspoons **vanilla extract**
150 g (5 oz) **red fruit yogurt**,
such as strawberry,
raspberry or cherry
100 g (½ oz) **fresh
raspberries** or **strawberries**,
cut into small pieces

Line a 12-section bun tray with paper cake cases. Put the flours, baking powder and sugar in a bowl.

Whisk together the eggs, oil, melted butter, vanilla extract and yogurt with a fork in a jug and add to the bowl.

Mix gently with a large metal spoon until the ingredients have started to blend together. Scatter with half the berry pieces and mix a little more until the ingredients are only just combined. Divide the muffin mixture between the paper cases. Scatter with the remaining berry pieces.

Bake in a preheated oven, 200°C (400°F), Gas Mark 6, for 15 minutes or until well risen and just firm. Transfer to a wire rack to cool.

For apple & sultana muffins, put 150 g (5 oz) plain flour, 50 g (2 oz) oatmeal, 2 teaspoons baking powder and 75 g (3 oz) golden caster sugar in a bowl and stir in 1 peeled, cored and diced dessert apple and 50 g (2 oz) sultanas. Whisk together the eggs, oil, melted butter and vanilla extract as above with 150 g (5 oz) apple- or vanilla-flavoured yogurt, add to the dry ingredients and mix together with a large metal spoon until only just combined. Divide between the paper cases and bake as above.

jelly bean cupcakes

Makes **12**
Preparation time **20 minutes**,
   plus cooling & setting
Cooking time **15–18 minutes**

150 g (5 oz) **plain flour**
150 g (5 oz) **caster sugar**
175 g (6 oz) **lightly salted
   butter**, plus extra for greasing
1½ teaspoons **baking
   powder**
1½ teaspoons **vanilla extract**
2 **eggs**

Icing
125 g (4 oz) **icing sugar**,
   sifted
½ teaspoon **vanilla extract**
about 4 teaspoons **water**
a few drops of **yellow**, **green**
   and **pink food colouring**
selection of **jelly beans**,
   to decorate

Line a 12-section bun tray with paper or foil cake cases. Put all the cake ingredients in a bowl and beat with a hand-held electric whisk for about a minute until light and creamy. Divide the cake mixture between the paper or foil cases.

Bake in a preheated oven, 180°C (350°F), Gas Mark 4, for 15–18 minutes or until well risen and just firm to the touch. Leave to cool in the tin.

Mix together the icing sugar, vanilla extract and enough water in a bowl to make a smooth icing. Divide the icing between 3 bowls and colour each batch with a different food colouring.

Remove the cakes from the tin, cover the tops with the different icings and decorate with jelly beans. Leave for 30 minutes for the icing to set.

For lemon swirl cupcakes, make the cake mixture as above, but add the finely grated rind of 1 lemon to the other ingredients before beating. Bake as above and leave to cool. Whip 150 ml (¼ pint) double cream with 1 tablespoon icing sugar until only just holding its shape. Spoon a little over each cake and swirl gently to the edges with the back of a teaspoon. Put a teaspoonful of lemon curd in the centre of each cake and scatter with 2–3 finely chopped green jelly sweets.

sleepy puppies

Makes **12**

Preparation time **45 minutes**, plus cooling

Cooking time **20 minutes**

125 g (4 oz) **lightly salted butter**, softened

125 g (4 oz) **caster sugar**

2 **eggs**

125 g (4 oz) **self-raising flour**

25 g (1 oz) **cocoa powder**

½ teaspoon **baking powder**

To decorate

75 g (3 oz) **unsalted butter**, softened

125 g (4 oz) **icing sugar**, plus extra for dusting

a few drops of **blue** and **black food colouring**

300 g (10 oz) **white ready-to-roll icing**

25 g (1 oz) **black ready-to-roll icing**

Line a 12-section bun tray with paper cake cases. Put all the cake ingredients in a bowl and beat with a hand-held electric whisk for about a minute until light and creamy. Divide the cake mixture between the paper cases.

Bake in a preheated oven, 180°C (350°F), Gas Mark 4, for 20 minutes or until risen and just firm to the touch. Transfer to a wire rack to cool.

Beat together the butter and icing sugar in a bowl until smooth and creamy. Beat in the blue food colouring and spread over the cakes using a small palette knife.

Take 25 g (1oz) of the white icing. Break off a little and reserve for the paws. Shape the remainder into a ball for the head and flatten slightly. Cut the reserved icing in half and shape 2 paws. Position over the side of one cupcake. Position the head so that it overlaps the paws. Shape 2 floppy ears in black icing and secure to the head using a dampened paintbrush. Repeat for the remaining cakes.

Use the black food colouring and a fine paintbrush to paint a nose, mouth, eye, patch and claws over each pup.

For cheeky cats, make and bake the cakes, then cover with the buttercream as above. Shape heads and paws in white ready-to-roll icing as above and position on the cakes. Shape small pointed ears using the white icing trimmings and secure in place with a dampened paintbrush. Paint eyes, noses, claws and patches of black markings using black food colouring, then mouths and the centres of the ears with pink food colouring. Cut fine strips of liquorice 'bootlace' and add for whiskers.

ducks, bunnies & chicks

Makes **12**

Preparation time **35 minutes**,
  plus cooling

Cooking time **20 minutes**

1 quantity **Buttercream**
  (see page 18)

a few drops of **yellow** and
  blue food colouring

12 **Vanilla Cupcakes**
  (see page 22)

2 **glacé cherries**

Put two-thirds of the buttercream in a bowl and beat in the yellow food colouring. Spread the buttercream in a flat layer over the tops of the cooled cakes using a small palette knife.

Colour the remaining buttercream with the blue food colouring. Put in a piping bag fitted with a writing nozzle, or use a paper piping bag with the merest tip snipped off (see page 15).

Pipe simple duck, bunny and chick shapes on to the buttercream-topped cakes. Cut the glacé cherries into thin slices and then into tiny triangles. Use to represent beaks on the ducks and chicks, and tiny eyes on the bunnies.

For Easter chick & egg cakes, make and bake the cakes as on page 22, but add the finely grated rind of 1 lemon to the cake ingredients. Leave to cool. Beat together 75 g (3 oz) softened unsalted butter, 125 g (4 oz) icing sugar and 2 teaspoons lemon juice until smooth. Spread over the tops of the cakes and position a mini yellow chick and several chocolate mini eggs on each.

pirate faces

Makes **12**
Preparation time **45 minutes**,
  plus cooling
Cooking time **20 minutes**

25 g (1 oz) **unsalted butter**,
  softened
50 g (2 oz) **icing sugar**, plus
  extra for dusting
a few drops of **red food
  colouring**
50 g (2 oz) **green
  ready-to-roll icing**
50 g (2 oz) **white
  ready-to-roll icing**
12 **Vanilla Cupcakes**
  (see page 22)
50 g (2 oz) **black
  ready-to-roll icing**
small **foil-wrapped chocolate
  coins**, to decorate (optional)

Beat together the butter and icing sugar in a bowl until smooth and creamy. Beat in the food colouring. Place in a piping bag fitted with a writing nozzle, or use a paper piping bag with the merest tip snipped off (see page 15).

Roll out the green icing on a work surface lightly dusted with icing sugar. Roll very thin ropes of white icing and position them about 5 mm (¼ inch) apart over the green icing. Gently roll with a rolling pin so that the ropes are flattened into the green icing to create a striped effect. Cut out little semicircular shapes and secure one to each cake to resemble a headscarf, using a little piped red buttercream to secure in place. Use the icing trimmings to shape knots on one side.

Shape eyes and smiling mouths from white icing and eye patches and pupils from black icing. Use the red buttercream in the bag to pipe wiggly lines for hair and around the mouths. Arrange on a plate, scattered with chocolate coins, if using.

For funny clown cakes, beat together 75 g (3 oz) softened unsalted butter and 125 g (4 oz) icing sugar until smooth. Thinly spread the cooled cakes with some of the buttercream. Colour the remainder with a few drops of yellow food colouring and use to pipe wiggly lines for hair as above. Shape balls of red ready-to-roll icing and position for noses, then add crosses of black ready-to-roll icing for eyes and large smiling mouths in red icing. Finish with large bow-ties cut from blue or green ready-to-roll icing.

reindeer cupcakes

Makes 12

Preparation time **40 minutes**,
  plus cooling & setting

Cooking time **25 minutes**

150 g (5 oz) **plain chocolate**,
  broken into pieces

1 tablespoon **cocoa powder**

1 tablespoon **boiling water**

50 g (2 oz) **unsalted butter**,
  softened

125 g (4 oz) **icing sugar**

12 **Chocolate Cupcakes**
  (see page 22)

6 **glacé cherries**

1 small packet of **candy-
  coated chocolate drops**

Melt the chocolate (see pages 16–17). Spoon the melted chocolate into a paper piping bag and snip off the merest tip (see page 15). Pipe lines of chocolate about 6 cm (2½ inches) long on a baking tray lined with nonstick baking parchment. Pipe on small branches for antlers. Make enough for 2 per cake, plus extras in case of breakages. Leave in a cool place, or refrigerate, to set.

Meanwhile, mix the cocoa powder with the boiling water in a large bowl. Add the butter and then gradually beat in the icing sugar to make a smooth icing. Spread the icing over the tops of the cooled cakes. Add a halved cherry for a nose and 2 little sweets for eyes, piping on the remaining melted chocolate to make pupils.

Peel the antlers off the baking parchment and stick at angles into the cakes. Store the cakes in a cool place until ready to serve.

For chocolate snowball cupcakes, make and bake the Vanilla Cupcakes as on page 22, but stir 50 g (2 oz) chopped white chocolate or chocolate chips into the cake mixture before baking. Beat together 75 g (3 oz) softened unsalted butter, 125 g (4 oz) icing sugar and 1 teaspoon boiling water until pale and creamy. Spread over the cooled cakes using a palette knife, peaking the mixture slightly. Press a white chocolate-covered honeycomb sweet into each cake and dust with icing sugar.

fruity flower cupcakes

Makes **12**
Preparation time **30 minutes**, plus cooling
Cooking time **20 minutes**

125 g (4 oz) **lightly salted butter**, softened
125 g (4 oz) **caster sugar**
2 **eggs**
150 g (5 oz) **self-raising flour**
½ teaspoon **baking powder**
50 g (2 oz) **semi-dried pineapple**, finely chopped
4 tablespoons **smooth apricot** or **red fruit jam**
2 x 100 g (3½ oz) pots **fruit-flavoured fromage frais**
¼ small **fresh pineapple**, peeled and cored
½ **mango**, stoned and peeled
handful of **fresh raspberries**, **blackberries** or **stoned cherries**
handful of **seedless black grapes**

Line a 12-section bun tray with paper cake cases. Put the butter, sugar, eggs, flour and baking powder in a bowl and beat with a hand-held electric whisk for about a minute until light and creamy. Divide the cake mixture between the paper cases and scatter with the semi-dried pineapple.

Bake in a preheated oven, 180°C (350°F), Gas Mark 4, for 20 minutes or until risen and just firm to the touch. Transfer to a wire rack to cool.

Spread each cake with a teaspoonful of the jam and then a thin layer of fromage frais.

Slice the fresh pineapple and mango. Cut rounds from the fruit flesh using a 2.5 cm (1 inch) cutter and arrange about 5 in a circle over each cake to make a flower shape. Place a raspberry, blackberry, cherry or grape in the centre of each, halving if large.

For strawberry cupcakes, make the cake mixture as above, but use 50 g (2 oz) dried strawberries in place of the semi-dried pineapple. Bake as above and leave to cool. Cut out a round from the centre top of each cake and spoon a little strawberry jam and strawberry-flavoured fromage frais into each cavity. Re-position the scooped out lids on top of the cakes and dust with icing sugar.

little devils' cakes

Makes **12**
Preparation time **15 minutes**,
 plus cooling & setting
Cooking time **10–15 minutes**

100 g (3½ oz) **lightly salted butter**, softened
100 g (3½ oz) **caster sugar**
a few drops of **vanilla extract**
2 **eggs**
100 g (3½ oz) **self-raising flour**
3 tablespoons **cocoa powder**
250 g (8 oz) **red ready-made fondant icing**
about 1 tablespoon **pre-boiled warm water**

Line a 12-section bun tray with paper cake cases. Put the butter, sugar and vanilla extract in a bowl and beat with a wooden spoon until light and creamy. Add the eggs and beat the mixture again, then sift in the flour and cocoa powder and stir in. Divide the cake mixture between the paper cases.

Bake in a preheated oven, 180°C (350°F), Gas Mark 4, for 10–15 minutes or until risen and firm to the touch. Transfer to a wire rack to cool.

Put about three-quarters of the icing in a bowl, add the water and stir until you have a thick but spreadable icing. When the cakes are cool, spread the icing over the tops with the back of a teaspoon or with a palette knife.

Roll small pieces of the remaining icing into devil's horns and then position them in the wet icing on top of the cakes. Leave to set.

For chocolate heart cakes, make and bake the cakes as above. Melt 100 g (3½ oz) milk chocolate with 15 g (½ oz) butter and 1 tablespoon milk (see pages 16–17). Stir until smooth, then spread over the cakes with a small palette knife. Melt 50 g (2 oz) white chocolate and pour on to a sheet of nonstick baking parchment. Spread in a thin layer and leave until set but not brittle. Cut out small heart shapes using a cutter and peel away the paper. Position a heart on each cake.

pumpkin heads

Makes **12**
Preparation time **30 minutes,**
  plus cooling
Cooking time **10–15 minutes**

100 g (3½ oz) **lightly salted
  butter**, softened
100 g (3½ oz) **caster sugar**
a few drops **vanilla extract**
2 **eggs**
100 g (3½ oz) **self-raising
  flour**

To decorate
125 g (4 oz) **red
  ready-to-roll icing**
125 g (4 oz) **yellow
  ready-to-roll icing**
125 g (4 oz) **green
  ready-to-roll icing**
125 g (4 oz) **black
  ready-to-roll icing**
black icing pen (optional)

Line a 12-section bun tray with paper cake cases. Put the butter, sugar and vanilla extract in a bowl and beat with a wooden spoon until light and creamy. Add the eggs and beat the mixture again, then sift in the flour and stir in. Divide the cake mixture between the paper cases.

Bake in a preheated oven, 180°C (350°F), Gas Mark 4, for 10–15 minutes or until risen and firm to the touch. Transfer to a wire rack to cool.

Knead together the red and the yellow icing to make orange icing. Roll a little piece of the green icing into a ball, then flatten into a round and gently push on to the top of a cake. Roll a larger piece of the orange icing into a ball. Place on top of the green 'pumpkin patch'. Roll a tiny piece of green icing into a stalk and push on to the top of the orange pumpkin. Use the black icing to make eyes and a crooked smile. Alternatively, draw the features on to the pumpkin head with a black icing pen.

For autumn leaf cakes, make and bake the cakes as above. Beat together 75 g (3 oz) softened unsalted butter, 125 g (4 oz) icing sugar, 1 teaspoon boiling water and a few drops of green food colouring. Spread over the cooled cakes, peaking with the back of a teaspoon. Roll 75 g (3 oz) each of chocolate-flavoured, light brown and yellow ready-to-roll icing out thinly on a work surface lightly dusted with icing sugar and cut out small leaf shapes using a knife or cutter. Mark veins with a knife and arrange over and around the cakes, bending them slightly so that they set in curved shapes.

birthday cake stack

Makes **18**

Preparation time **25 minutes**, plus cooling

Cooking time **20 minutes**

175 g (6 oz) **lightly salted butter**, softened

175 g (6 oz) **golden caster sugar**

3 **eggs**

200 g (7 oz) **self-raising flour**

1 teaspoon **baking powder**

finely grated **rind** of 2 **lemons**

To decorate

125 g (4 oz) **unsalted butter**, softened

200 g (7 oz) **icing sugar**

a few drops of **pink** or **blue food colouring**

125 g (4 oz) small **sweets**, such as dolly mixtures and jellies

sugar sprinkles (optional)

birthday candles and **candleholders**

Line 18 sections of 2 x 12-section bun trays with paper cake cases. Put all the cake ingredients in a bowl and beat with a hand-held electric whisk for about a minute until light and creamy. Divide the cake mixture between the paper cases.

Bake in a preheated oven, 180°C (350°F), Gas Mark 4, for 20 minutes or until risen and just firm to the touch. Transfer to a wire rack to cool.

Beat together the unsalted butter and icing sugar in a bowl until smooth and creamy. Beat in the food colouring. Spread the buttercream over the cooled cakes using a small palette knife. Decorate the cakes with plenty of small sweets and sugar sprinkles, if using.

Arrange a layer of cakes on a serving plate and stack another 2 or 3 tiers on top. Push the required amount of birthday candles and candleholders into the cakes.

For chocolate cake stack, make the cake mixture as above, but use 40 g (1½ oz) cocoa powder in place of 40 g (1½ oz) of the flour. Bake as above. Beat together 125 g (4 oz) softened unsalted butter and 200 g (7 oz) icing sugar until smooth. Blend 40 g (1½ oz) cocoa powder with 5 tablespoons boiling water and beat into the buttercream mixture. Spread over the cooled cakes. Scatter the cakes with 125 g (4 oz) small chocolate sweets, such as chopped chocolate-covered honeycomb, candy-covered chocolate drops and chocolate polka dots. Scatter with chocolate sprinkles before stacking as above.

number cakes

Makes **12**

Preparation time **25 minutes**, plus cooling

Cooking time **20 minutes**

a few drops of **green** or **yellow food colouring**

1 quantity **Buttercream** (see page 18)

12 **Vanilla Cupcakes** (see page 22)

175 g (6 oz) **white ready-to-roll icing**

icing sugar, for dusting

50 g (2 oz) **red ready-to-roll icing**

50 g (2 oz) **blue ready-to-roll icing**

coloured sugar strands

Beat the food colouring into the buttercream and then spread all over the tops of the cooled cakes using a small palette knife.

Knead the white icing on a work surface lightly dusted with icing sugar, then roll out. Cut out 12 rounds using a 6 cm (2½ inch) cookie cutter and gently press one on to the top of each cake.

Roll out the red icing and cut out numbers of your choice for 6 of the cakes using a small, sharp knife or alphabet cutters. Secure to the cakes with a dampened paintbrush. Cut out the remaining numbers from the blue icing.

Brush the edges of the white icing with a dampened paintbrush and scatter over the sugar strands.

For party 'name' cakes, make the buttercream as above, omitting the food colouring, and reserve 4 tablespoons. Spread the remainder over the cooled cakes, smoothing it as flat as possible with a small palette knife. Colour the reserved buttercream with a few drops of red food colouring (or a colour of your choice), put in a paper piping bag and snip off the merest tip (see page 15). Pipe names or initials over the cakes. Put several clear boiled sweets in a polythene bag and crush with a rolling pin. Scatter around the edges of the cakes.

cupcakes
for adults

marsala raisin & ricotta cakes

Makes **12**

Preparation time **20 minutes,**
plus cooling

Cooking time **25 minutes**

100 g (3½ oz) **raisins**
75 ml (3 fl oz) **Marsala** or
dry sherry
125 g (4 oz) **lightly salted**
butter, softened
100 g (3½ oz) **light**
muscovado sugar
1 teaspoon **vanilla extract**
2 **eggs**
150 g (5 oz) **self-raising flour**
½ teaspoon **baking powder**

Frosting
250 g (8 oz) **ricotta cheese**
50 g (2 oz) **icing sugar**

To decorate
handful of **flaked almonds**,
lightly toasted
12 **raisins**

Line a 12-section bun tray with paper cake cases. Put the raisins in a small saucepan with the Marsala or sherry and heat until bubbling around the edge. Simmer for 1 minute, then remove from the heat and turn into a bowl. Leave to cool.

Put the butter, muscovado sugar, vanilla extract, eggs, flour and baking powder in a separate bowl and beat with a hand-held electric whisk for about a minute until light and creamy.

Drain the raisins thoroughly, reserving the unabsorbed Marsala or sherry, and stir into the cake mixture. Divide between the cake cases.

Bake in a preheated oven, 180°C (350°F), Gas Mark 4, for 20 minutes or until risen and just firm. Transfer to a wire rack to cool.

Put the ricotta in a bowl and gently stir in 1 teaspoon of the reserved Marsala or sherry and the icing sugar – don't overbeat the mixture or it will become too runny.

Pierce the tops of the cakes with a skewer and drizzle with the remaining Marsala or sherry. Spread the ricotta mixture on top. Use the flaked almonds and raisins to decorate each cake with a simple flower shape.

For rum & raisin cheesecakes, soak 100 g (3½ oz) raisins in 3 tablespoons rum for several hours until absorbed. Make the cake mixture as above, but replace the Marsala or sherry-soaked raisins with the rum-soaked raisins. Bake as above. Beat 200 g (7 oz) cream cheese with 40 g (1½ oz) icing sugar and spread over the cakes. Scatter with crushed digestive biscuits.

hot & spicy cupcakes

Makes **12**
Preparation time **15 minutes**,
  plus cooling
Cooking time **25 minutes**

1 **medium-strength red chilli**,
  deseeded and finely
  chopped, plus 6 small **red
  chillies**, halved lengthways
125 g (4 oz) **lightly salted
  butter**, softened
175 g (6 oz) **caster sugar**
2 **eggs**
150 g (5 oz) **self-raising flour**
½ teaspoon **baking powder**
125 g (4 oz) **soft dried
  mango**, chopped
2 tablespoons **water**
5 tablespoons **vodka**
75 g **icing sugar**
finely grated **rind** of 1 **lime**,
  to sprinkle

Line a 12-section bun tray with paper cake cases.
Put the chopped chilli, butter, 125 g (4 oz) of the caster
sugar, the eggs, flour and baking powder in a bowl and
beat with a hand-held electric whisk for about a minute
until light and creamy.

Stir in the mango and then divide the cake mixture
between the paper cases. Place a halved chilli across
the top of each cake.

Bake in a preheated oven, 180°C (350°F), Gas Mark 4,
for 20 minutes or until risen and just firm to the touch.
Transfer to a wire rack to cool.

Put the remaining caster sugar in a small saucepan
with the water and heat gently until the sugar has
dissolved. Bring to the boil and boil for 3–4 minutes
until thickened and syrupy. Stir in 4 tablespoons of the
vodka (taking care as the mixture will splutter) and heat
until smooth.

Pierce the tops of the cakes with a skewer and drizzle
the syrup over. Blend the remaining vodka with the
icing sugar to make a thin paste and drizzle over the
cakes. Sprinkle with the lime zest.

For iced fresh ginger cupcakes, peel and finely
grate 50 g (2 oz) fresh root ginger, working over a
bowl to catch the juice. Make the cake mixture as
above, adding the grated ginger in place of the
chopped chilli, reserving the ginger juice. Bake as
above. Once the cakes are cool, mix the ginger juice
with 75 g (3 oz) icing sugar to make a thin glacé
icing, adding a dash of lemon juice if the mixture
is too dry. Use to decorate the cakes.

almond praline cupcakes

Makes **12**
Preparation time **30 minutes,**
 plus cooling
Cooking time **25 minutes**

sunflower oil, for brushing
250 g (8 oz) **caster sugar**
100 ml (3½ fl oz) **water**
75 g (3 oz) **flaked almonds**
125 g (4 oz) **lightly salted
 butter**, softened
1 teaspoon **vanilla extract**
2 **eggs**
150 g (5 oz) **self-raising flour**
½ teaspoon **baking powder**

Frosting
75 g (3 oz) **unsalted butter,**
 softened
125 g (4 oz) **icing sugar**
1 teaspoon **hot water**

Line a 12-section bun tray with paper cake cases. Brush a baking sheet lightly with oil. Put 150 g (5 oz) of the caster sugar in a small, heavy based saucepan with the water and heat gently until it has dissolved. Bring to the boil and boil rapidly until the syrup has turned to a pale golden caramel. Immediately stir in the flaked almonds. When coated, turn out on to the prepared baking sheet, spread in a thin layer and leave until cold and brittle.

Snap half the praline into jagged pieces and reserve. Process the remainder in a food processor until ground.

Put the butter, remaining caster sugar, vanilla extract, eggs, flour and baking powder in a bowl and beat with a hand-held electric whisk for about a minute until light and creamy. Stir in the ground praline. Divide the cake mixture between the paper cases.

Bake in a preheated oven, 180°C (350°F), Gas Mark 4, for 20 minutes or until risen and just firm to the touch. Transfer to a wire rack to cool.

Beat together the butter and icing sugar with the hot water in a bowl until pale and creamy. Spread over the cakes using a small palette knife. Decorate with the praline pieces.

For maple & pecan praline cakes, make the praline as above, but use 75 g (3 oz) pecan nuts instead of the almonds. Grind half the praline in a food processor. Make the cake mixture as above, adding the ground pecan praline. Bake as above. Whip 150 ml (¼ pint) double cream with 3 tablespoons maple syrup until just holding its shape. Spoon over the cooled cakes. Scatter with the praline pieces.

strawberry marguerita cupcakes

Makes 12

Preparation time **25 minutes**, plus soaking & cooling

Cooking time **20 minutes**

75 g (3 oz) **dried strawberries**

6 tablespoons **tequila**

125 g (4 oz) **lightly salted butter**, softened

125 g (4 oz) **caster sugar**

finely grated **rind** and **juice** of 1 **lime**

2 **eggs**

150 g (5 oz) **self-raising flour**

½ teaspoon **baking powder**

To finish

50 g (2 oz) **caster sugar**

a few drops of **red food colouring**

150 ml (¼ pint) **double cream**

12 **fresh strawberries**

Line a 12-section bun tray with paper cake cases. Chop the dried strawberries roughly and put in a small bowl with the tequila. Cover and leave to soak for at least 2 hours so that the strawberries plump up.

Drain the strawberries, reserving the tequila. Put the butter, sugar, lime rind, eggs, flour and baking powder in a bowl and beat with a hand-held electric whisk for about a minute until light and creamy. Stir in the strawberries. Divide the cake mixture between the paper cases.

Bake in a preheated oven, 180°C (350°F), Gas Mark 4, for 20 minutes or until risen and just firm to the touch. Transfer to a wire rack to cool.

Put the sugar in a small bowl and add the food colouring. Work the colouring into the sugar using the back of a teaspoon. Brush the edges of the cakes with a little lime juice and roll the rims in the coloured sugar. Mix the remaining lime juice with the reserved tequila. Pierce the cakes all over with a skewer and drizzle over the juice mixture.

Whip the cream until just beginning to hold its shape and pipe or spoon over the cakes. Decorate each with a whole fresh strawberry.

For piña colada cupcakes, omit the strawberries and tequila and make the cake mixture as above, but add 25 g (1 oz) grated creamed coconut to the ingredients before beating, then stir in 75 g (3 oz) chopped semi-dried pineapple. Bake as above. Lightly whip 150 ml (¼ pint) double cream with 3 tablespoons white rum and spoon over the cooled cakes. Decorate with fresh pineapple wedges.

mini minted cupcakes

Makes **50**

Preparation time **45 minutes**, plus cooling

Cooking time **12 minutes**

50 g (2 oz) **extra-strong mints** (about 1¼ tubes)

125 g (4 oz) **lightly salted butter**, softened

75 g (3 oz) **caster sugar**

2 **eggs**

125 g (4 oz) **self-raising flour**

½ teaspoon **baking powder**

To decorate

100 g (3½ oz) **plain chocolate**, chopped

25 g (1 oz) **milk chocolate**, chopped

Stand 50 mini paper or foil cake (petit four) cases on a baking sheet. Put the mints in a polythene bag and beat with a rolling pin to break them into a coarse crumb.

Tip the mints into a bowl and add all the remaining cake ingredients. Beat with a hand-held electric whisk for about a minute until light and creamy. Divide the cake mixture between the paper cases.

Bake in a preheated oven, 180°C (350°F), Gas Mark 4, for 12 minutes or until risen and just firm to the touch. Transfer to a wire rack to cool.

Melt the plain and milk chocolate in separate bowls (see pages 16–17). Put the melted milk chocolate in a paper piping bag and snip off the merest tip (see page 15). Spread the plain chocolate over the cakes. Use the milk chocolate to scribble lines back and forth over the plain chocolate or little dots. Leave in a cool place to set before serving.

For mini mint fudge cakes, make the cake mixture as above, but substitute 15 g (½ oz) cocoa powder for 15 g (½ oz) of the flour. Bake as above. Melt 200 g (7 oz) white chocolate with 4 tablespoons milk, stirring until smooth. Stir in 150 g (5 oz) icing sugar. Spread over the cooled cakes and dust with cocoa powder.

frangipane & apricot cupcakes

Makes **12**
Preparation time **30 minutes**,
  plus cooling
Cooking time **25 minutes**

150 g (5 oz) **dried apricots**,
  sliced
5 tablespoons **brandy**
3 tablespoons **water**
5 tablespoons **apricot jam**
100 g (3½ oz) **almond paste**
icing sugar, for dusting
125 g (4 oz) **lightly salted
  butter**, softened
75 g (3 oz) **caster sugar**
2 **eggs**
150 g (5 oz) **self-raising flour**
½ teaspoon **baking powder**
50 g (2 oz) **ground almonds**
1 teaspoon **almond extract**

Line a 12-section bun tray with paper cake cases.
Cook the apricot slices gently in the brandy and water
in a small saucepan for 4–5 minutes until plumped up
slightly and most of the liquid has been absorbed. Press
the jam through a sieve into the pan and leave to cool.

Roll out the almond paste on a work surface lightly
dusted with icing sugar. Cut out small heart shapes
using a cutter, about 2.5 cm (1 inch) in diameter.
Gather the remaining almond paste into a ball. Place
the hearts on a baking sheet lined with baking
parchment and heat under a preheated moderate grill,
watching closely, until beginning to toast. Leave to cool.

Put all the remaining ingredients in a bowl. Grate in
the remaining almond paste and beat with a hand-held
electric whisk for about a minute until light and creamy.
Divide between the paper cases.

Bake in a preheated oven, 180°C (350°F), Gas Mark 4,
for 20 minutes or until risen and just firm to the touch.
Transfer to a wire rack to cool.

Pile teaspoonfuls of the apricot mixture on to the cakes
and position a heart on top. Serve dusted with icing sugar.

For mini linzer cakes, beat together 125 g (4 oz)
softened lightly salted butter, 125 g (4 oz) caster
sugar, 125 g (4 oz) self-raising flour, ½ teaspoon
baking powder, 50 g (2 oz) ground almonds, 2 eggs
and 1 teaspoon almond extract until light and creamy.
Spoon into the paper cases and bake as above.
Once cooled, top each with 1 tablespoon raspberry
jam and scatter with toasted flaked almonds. Dust with
icing sugar.

lavender cupcakes

Makes **12**

Preparation time **20 minutes**, plus cooling

Cooking time **20 minutes**

6 **lavender flowers**, plus extra small **sprigs** to decorate
125 g (4 oz) **lightly salted butter**, softened
125 g (4 oz) **caster sugar**
finely grated **rind** of ½ **orange**
2 **eggs**
150 g (5 oz) **self-raising flour**
½ teaspoon **baking powder**

Icing
150 g (5 oz) **icing sugar**
4–5 teaspoons **orange juice**
a few drops of **lilac food colouring**

Line a 12-section bun tray with paper cake cases. Pull the lavender flowers from their stems and put in a bowl with the butter, caster sugar, orange rind, eggs, flour and baking powder. Beat with a hand-held electric whisk for about a minute until light and creamy. Divide the cake mixture between the paper cases.

Bake in a preheated oven, 180°C (350°F), Gas Mark 4, for 20 minutes or until risen and just firm to the touch. Transfer to a wire rack to cool.

Mix the icing sugar with enough orange juice in a bowl to make a thin glacé icing. Colour with the food colouring. Spread over the cakes and decorate with small sprigs of lavender flowers.

For sweet thyme cupcakes, finely chop several lemon thyme sprigs. Make the cake mixture as above, but use the lemon thyme in place of the lavender and the finely grated rind of 1 lemon instead of the orange rind. Bake as above. Whip 150 ml (¼ pint) double cream with 2 tablespoons almond-flavoured liqueur or clear honey and spread over the cooled cakes. Decorate with lemon thyme sprigs.

pink rose cupcakes

Makes **12**

Preparation time **20 minutes**, plus cooling

Cooking time **20 minutes**

25 g (1 oz) **sugared rose petals**, plus extra to decorate

125 g (4 oz) **caster sugar**

125 g (4 oz) **lightly salted butter**, softened

2 **eggs**

150 g (5 oz) **self-raising flour**

½ teaspoon **baking powder**

1 tablespoon **rosewater**

Frosting

250 g (8 oz) **mascarpone cheese**

125 g (4 oz) **icing sugar**

1 teaspoon **lemon juice**

a few drops of **pink food colouring** (optional)

Line a 12-section bun tray with paper cake cases. Put the sugared rose petals and caster sugar in a food processor and process until the rose petals are chopped into small pieces. Tip into a bowl and add all the remaining cake ingredients. Beat with a hand-held electric whisk for about a minute until light and creamy. Divide the cake mixture between the cake cases.

Bake in a preheated oven, 180°C (350°F), Gas Mark 4, for 20 minutes or until risen and just firm to the touch. Transfer to a wire rack to cool.

Beat together the mascarpone, icing sugar, lemon juice and food colouring, if using, with a wooden spoon in a bowl until smooth. Spread over the tops of the cakes using a small palette knife and decorate with extra sugared rose petals.

For frosted blueberry cupcakes, put 1 teaspoon egg white in a bowl with 75 g (3 oz) fresh blueberries and stir until the berries are coated in a thin film of egg white. Roll in a little caster sugar until coated. Make the cake mixture as above, but omit the sugared rose petals and rosewater and add 1 teaspoon vanilla bean paste or vanilla extract. Bake as above. Make the frosting as above, but use a few drops of lilac food colouring instead of the pink food colouring. Spread over the tops of the cooled cakes. Arrange the frosted blueberries on top.

pistachio cream cupcakes

Makes **12**
Preparation time **40 minutes**,
   plus cooling
Cooking time **20 minutes**

150 g (5 oz) **pistachio nuts**
125 g (4 oz) **lightly salted
   butter**, softened
125 g (4 oz) **caster sugar**
2 **eggs**
150 g (5 oz) **self-raising flour**
½ teaspoon **baking powder**

To decorate
300 ml (½ pint) **double
   cream**
2 tablespoons **icing sugar**,
   plus extra for dusting
2 tablespoons **almond-** or
   orange-flavoured liqueur

Line a 12-section bun tray with paper cake cases.
Put the pistachio nuts in a heatproof bowl, cover with
boiling water and leave to stand for 30 seconds. Drain
thoroughly and rub between several thicknesses of
kitchen paper to loosen the skins. Peel away the skins
– you needn't be too thorough about this, as long as
most of the skins are removed. Process in a food
processor until finely chopped.

Beat the butter, caster sugar, eggs, flour, baking powder
and 50 g (2 oz) of the ground nuts with a hand-held
electric whisk in a bowl for about a minute until light and
creamy. Divide the mixture between the paper cases.

Bake in a preheated oven, 180°C (350°F), Gas Mark 4,
for 20 minutes or until risen and just firm to the touch.
Transfer to a wire rack to cool.

Peel away the paper cases. Whip the cream with the
icing sugar and liqueur in a bowl until only just holding
its shape. Transfer half to a separate bowl and reserve.
Spread the remainder around the cakes and roll in the
remaining ground nuts to coat the sides. Spoon the
reserved flavoured cream on top.

For macadamia & raspberry cupcakes, finely chop
50 g (2 oz) macadamia nuts and lightly toast in a dry
frying pan. Leave to cool. Make the cake mixture as
above, but use the macadamia nuts in place of the
ground pistachio nuts. Bake as above. Once cooled,
split the cakes in half horizontally. Lightly whip 150 ml
(¼ pint) double cream with 1 tablespoon icing sugar.
Sandwich the cakes together with the cream and
fresh raspberries. Serve dusted with icing sugar.

sweet camomile muffins

Makes **12**
Preparation time **15 minutes**
Cooking time **15–18 minutes**

15 g (½ oz) **camomile tea**
  (either loose leaf or from
  bags)
75 g (3 oz) **ground almonds**
100 g (3½ oz) **golden
  caster sugar**
275 g (9 oz) **plain flour**
1 tablespoon **baking powder**
finely grated **rind** of 1 **lemon**
75 g (3 oz) **sultanas**
75 g (3 oz) **lightly salted
  butter**, melted, plus extra
  to serve
2 **eggs**, beaten
284 ml (9½ fl oz) carton
  buttermilk

Line a 12-section muffin tray with paper muffin cases. Put the tea, ground almonds and sugar in a food processor and process briefly until combined. Turn into a bowl and stir in the flour, baking powder, lemon rind and sultanas.

Mix together the melted butter, eggs and buttermilk in a separate bowl and add to the flour mixture. Use a large metal spoon to stir the ingredients together until only just combined. Divide the muffin mixture between the paper cases.

Bake in a preheated oven, 220°C (425°F), Gas Mark 7, for 15–18 minutes or until risen and pale golden. Serve warm, split and buttered.

For peppermint tea & white chocolate muffins,
process the ingredients in a food processor as above, but use 15 g (½ oz) peppermint tea in place of the camomile tea. Mix with the dry ingredients as above, but omit the sultanas and stir in 100 g (3½ oz) chopped white chocolate. Combine with the wet ingredients and bake as above.

florentine cupcakes

Makes **12**

Preparation time **20 minutes**, plus cooling

Cooking time **30 minutes**

sunflower oil, for brushing

75 g (3 oz) **flaked almonds**

50 g (2 oz) **sultanas**

125 g (4 oz) **glacé cherries**, quartered

4 tablespoons **golden syrup**

12 **Vanilla Cupcakes** (see page 22)

50 g (2 oz) **plain chocolate**, broken into pieces

Brush a baking sheet lightly with oil. Beat together the flaked almonds, sultanas, glacé cherries and golden syrup in a bowl. Tip the mixture out on to the prepared baking sheet and spread in a thin layer.

Bake in a preheated oven, 200°C (400°F), Gas Mark 6, for 8 minutes or until the nuts and syrup are turning golden. Remove from the oven and leave to cool slightly.

Break up the mixture and scatter over the cooled cupcakes in an even layer.

Melt the chocolate (see pages 16–17) and then put in a piping bag fitted with a writing nozzle. Scribble lines of chocolate across the fruit and nut topping. Leave to set before serving.

For toffee crunch cupcakes, make and bake 12 Chocolate Cupcakes as on page 22. Gently heat 50 g (2 oz) unsalted butter, 50 g (2 oz) caster sugar and 2 tablespoons golden syrup in a small saucepan until the butter has melted. Increase the heat and cook until the mixture starts to turn golden around the edge. Immediately stir in 100 g (3½ oz) crisp rice cereal and then spoon on to the cakes. Leave to cool before serving.

red velvet cupcakes

Makes **12**

Preparation time **20 minutes**,
   plus cooling

Cooking time **20–25 minutes**

150 g (5 oz) **self-raising flour**

2 tablespoons **cocoa powder**

½ teaspoon **bicarbonate
   of soda**

100 ml (3½ fl oz) **buttermilk**

1 teaspoon vinegar

**50 g (2 oz) lightly salted
   butter**, softened

100 g (3½ oz) **caster sugar**

1 egg

50 g (2 oz) **raw beetroot**,
   peeled and finely grated

Frosting

200 g (7 oz) **full-fat cream
   cheese**

2 teaspoons **vanilla extract**

300 g (10 oz) **icing sugar**

12 **fresh cherries**, to decorate

Line a 12-section muffin tray with paper muffin cases.
Combine the flour, cocoa powder and bicarbonate of
soda in a bowl. Mix together the buttermilk and vinegar
in a jug.

Beat together the butter and caster sugar in a separate
bowl until pale and creamy, then beat in the egg and
beetroot.

Sift half the flour mixture into the bowl and stir in gently
with a large metal spoon. Stir in half the buttermilk
mixture. Sift and stir in the remaining flour mixture, then
the remaining liquid. Divide the muffin mixture between
the paper cases.

Bake in a preheated oven, 180°C (350°F), Gas Mark 4,
for 20–25 minutes or until risen and just firm to the touch.
Transfer to a wire rack to cool.

Beat the cream cheese with a wooden spoon in a
bowl until softened. Beat in the vanilla extract and icing
sugar until smooth. Swirl over the tops of the cakes and
decorate each with a cherry.

For spicy pear & goats' cheese cupcakes, make the
cake mixture as above, but replace the cocoa powder
with an additional 2 tablespoons self-raising flour and
add 1 teaspoon ground mixed spice, and then omit
the beetroot. Stir in 75 g (3 oz) chopped dried pears
into the mixture before baking as above. Beat together
100 g (3½ oz) soft mild goats' cheese with 150 g
(5 oz) icing sugar and 1 teaspoon lemon juice.
Spread over the tops of the cakes (omit the cherries).

marmalade madeira cupcakes

Makes **12**
Preparation time **15 minutes**
Cooking time **20 minutes**

150 g (5 oz) **lightly salted butter**, softened
75 g (3 oz) **caster sugar**
75 g (3 oz) **orange marmalade**
2 **eggs**
175 g (6 oz) **self-raising flour**
½ teaspoon **baking powder**
1 teaspoon **vanilla extract**
piece of **candied orange peel**

Line a 12-section muffin tray with paper muffin cases. Put the butter, sugar, marmalade, eggs, flour, baking powder and vanilla extract in a bowl and beat with a hand-held electric whisk for about a minute until light and creamy. Divide the cake mixture between the paper cases.

Cut thin strips from the candied orange peel and lay a couple of slices over each cupcake.

Bake in a preheated oven, 180°C (350°F), Gas Mark 4, for 20 minutes or until risen and just firm to the touch. Transfer to a wire rack to cool.

For ginger spice Madeira cupcakes, make the cake mixture as above, but use 75 g (3 oz) ginger marmalade instead of the orange marmalade and add 1 teaspoon ground ginger. Divide the mixture between the paper cases. Thinly slice 25 g (1 oz) crystallized ginger pieces and arrange over the cakes before baking as above.

coffee & walnut cupcakes

Makes **12**

Preparation time **20 minutes**,
plus cooling

Cooking time **20 minutes**

2 teaspoons **espresso
coffee powder**
2 teaspoons **boiling water**
125 g (4 oz) **lightly salted
butter**, softened
125 g (4 oz) **golden
caster sugar**
2 **eggs**
150 g (5 oz) **self-raising flour**
½ teaspoon **baking powder**
50 g (2 oz) **chopped walnuts**

Coffee buttercream
1 teaspoon **espresso
coffee powder**
2 teaspoons **boiling water**
100 g (3½ oz) **unsalted
butter**, softened
150 g (5 oz) **golden
icing sugar**
12 **walnut halves**, to decorate

Line a 12-section bun tray with paper cake cases.
Blend the coffee powder with the boiling water. Put the
butter, caster sugar, eggs, flour and baking powder in a
bowl. Add the coffee and beat with a hand-held electric
whisk for about a minute until light and creamy. Stir in
the chopped walnuts. Divide the cake mixture between
the paper cases.

Bake in a preheated oven, 180°C (350°F), Gas Mark 4,
for 20 minutes or until risen and just firm to the touch.
Transfer to a wire rack to cool.

Blend the coffee powder with the boiling water for the
buttercream. Beat with the butter and icing sugar in a
bowl until pale and creamy.

Spread the buttercream over the cakes using a small
palette knife. Alternatively, put in a piping bag fitted
with a star nozzle and pipe swirls over the tops of the
cakes. Decorate each with a walnut half.

For crunchy peanut cupcakes, beat 75 g (3 oz)
softened lightly salted butter, 125 g (4 oz) crunchy
peanut butter, 125 g (4 oz) caster sugar, 2 eggs,
150 g (5 oz) self-raising flour, ½ teaspoon baking
powder and 1 tablespoon milk with a hand-held
electric whisk for about a minute until light and creamy.
Divide between the paper cases and bake as above.
Make the buttercream as above, but omit the coffee
powder and water, and spread over the tops of the
cooled cakes. Scatter with chopped peanuts.

spiced sweet potato cupcakes

Makes **9**
Preparation time **25 minutes**,
  plus cooling
Cooking time **35 minutes**

125 g (4 oz) **sweet potato**
  (about **1** small)
10 **cardamom pods**
50 g (2 oz) **lightly salted**
  butter
6 tablespoons **clear honey**
2 **eggs**, beaten
100 g (3½ oz) **self-raising**
  flour
½ teaspoon **baking powder**
3 tablespoons **flaked**
  almonds, toasted
50 g (2 oz) **golden**
  icing sugar
2 teaspoons **lemon juice**

Line 9 sections of a 12-section bun tray with paper cake cases. Scrub the sweet potato and cut into chunks. Cook in a saucepan of boiling water for 10 minutes or until tender. Drain well and return to the pan. Mash until smooth and leave to cool.

Crush the cardamom pods in a mortar with a pestle to release the seeds. Discard the shells and crush the seeds as finely as possible.

Melt the butter in a small saucepan with the honey. Turn into a bowl and leave to cool slightly. Beat in the sweet potato and cardamom, then the eggs, flour and baking powder.

Divide the cake mixture between the paper cases and scatter with the flaked almonds.

Bake in a preheated oven, 180°C (350°F), Gas Mark 4, for 20 minutes or until risen and just firm. Transfer to a wire rack to cool.

Beat the sugar with the lemon juice in a bowl to make a smooth, thin glacé icing. Drizzle thin lines of icing back and forth across the cakes.

For spicy parsnip cakes, make the cake mixture as above, but use 125 g (4 oz) mashed parsnip instead of the sweet potato and ¼ teaspoon hot chilli powder instead of the cardamom. Spoon into the paper cases and scatter with 2 tablespoons pine nuts. Bake as above. Dust lightly with icing sugar before serving.

raspberry amaretti cakes

Makes **12**

Preparation time **20 minutes**,
  plus cooling

Cooking time **20 minutes**

75 g (3 oz) **amaretti biscuits**

75 g (3 oz) **light
  muscovado sugar**

100 g (3½ oz) **lightly salted
  butter**, softened

2 **eggs**

75 g (3 oz) **self-raising flour**

½ teaspoon **baking powder**

Topping

200 g (7 oz) **cream cheese**

8 tablespoons **icing sugar**,
  plus extra for dusting

250 g (8 oz) **fresh
  raspberries**

Line a 12-section bun tray with paper cake cases.
Put the amaretti biscuits in a polythene bag and crush
with a rolling pin.

Tip the crushed biscuits into a bowl and add the
muscovado sugar, butter, eggs, flour and baking
powder. Beat with a hand-held electric whisk for about
a minute until pale and creamy. Divide the cake mixture
between the paper cases.

Bake in a preheated oven, 180°C (350°F), Gas Mark 4,
for 20 minutes or until risen and just firm to the touch.
Transfer to a wire rack to cool.

Beat the cream cheese with a wooden spoon in a bowl
to soften, then beat in the icing sugar. Spread over the
tops of the cakes with a small palette knife. Arrange a
layer of raspberries on top and dust with icing sugar.

For apricot & almond cupcakes, make the cake
mixture as above. Roughly chop 50 g (2 oz) ready-to-
eat dried apricots and 50 g (2 oz) whole blanched
almonds and mix together. Scatter about a third into
the cake mixture and lightly stir in, then spoon the
mixture into the paper cases. Scatter the remainder
over the tops and bake as above. Serve dusted with
icing sugar.

lemon meringue cupcakes

Makes **12**
Preparation time **20 minutes**
Cooking time **25 minutes**

125 g (4 oz) **lightly salted butter**, softened
125 g (4 oz) **caster sugar**
2 **eggs**
150 g (5 oz) **self-raising flour**
½ teaspoon **baking powder**
1 teaspoon **vanilla extract**
finely grated **rind** of 1 **lemon**

Topping & filling
2 **egg whites**
100 g (3½ oz) **caster sugar**
4 tablespoons **lemon curd**

Line a 12-section bun tray with paper cake cases. Put all the cake ingredients in a bowl and beat with a hand-held electric whisk for about a minute until light and creamy. Divide the cake mixture between the paper cases.

Bake in a preheated oven, 180°C (350°F), Gas Mark 4, for 20 minutes or until risen and just firm to the touch.

Meanwhile, beat the egg whites in a thoroughly clean bowl until peaking. Gradually beat in the sugar, a tablespoonful at a time, to make a firm, glossy meringue.

Remove the cakes from the oven and raise the temperature to 230°C (450°F), Gas Mark 8.

Scoop out about 1 teaspoon of sponge from the top of each cake and fill with the lemon curd. Pile up the meringue on top, swirling it with a palette knife. Return to the oven for a further 1–2 minutes, watching closely, until the meringue is beginning to brown. Serve warm.

For mini iced Alaskas, make and bake the cakes as above and leave to cool. Make the meringue as above. Take a small scoop of sponge out of the centre of each cake and put ½ teaspoon raspberry or strawberry jam and 1 teaspoon vanilla ice cream into each. Spread the meringue on top so that the ice cream is completely covered. Return to the oven at the raised temperature and lightly brown as above. Serve immediately.

espresso cream cakes

Makes **12**

Preparation time **20 minutes**, plus cooling

Cooking time **20 minutes**

150 g (5 oz) **lightly salted butter**, softened

150 g (5 oz) **caster sugar**

175 g (6 oz) **self-raising flour**

1 tablespoon **espresso** or **strong coffee powder**

3 **eggs**

1 teaspoon **vanilla extract**

To finish

4 tablespoons **coffee-flavoured liqueur**

300 ml (½ pint) **double cream**

75 g (3 oz) piece of **plain** or **milk chocolate**

cocoa or **drinking chocolate powder**, for dusting

Line a 12-section bun tray with paper cake cases. Put all the cake ingredients in a bowl and beat with a hand-held electric whisk for 1–2 minutes until light and creamy. Divide the cake mixture evenly between the paper cases.

Bake in a preheated oven, 180°C (350°F), Gas Mark 4, for 20 minutes or until risen and just firm to the touch. Transfer to a wire rack to cool.

Drizzle the cooled cupcakes with 2 tablespoons of the coffee-flavoured liqueur.

Put the remaining liqueur in a bowl with the cream and whip until the cream is thickened and only just holds its shape. Spread the cream over the tops of the cakes using a small palette knife, swirling it right to the edges.

Pare curls from the piece of chocolate using a vegetable peeler – if the chocolate breaks off in small, brittle shards, try softening it in the microwave for a few seconds first, but take care not to overheat and melt it. Scatter the chocolate curls over the cakes and dust with a little cocoa or drinking chocolate powder. Store the cakes in a cool place until ready to serve.

For liqueur-drizzled mocha cakes, toast 40 g (1½ oz) flaked almonds and mix with 1 tablespoon caster sugar and ¼ teaspoon ground cinnamon. Make the cake mixture as above and divide between the paper cases. Scatter with half the almond mixture and then bake as above. Drizzle each cake with ½ teaspoon coffee-flavoured liqueur and scatter with the remaining almond mixture. Return to the oven for 3 minutes, then transfer to a wire rack to cool.

savoury cupcakes

corn, chilli & bacon muffins

Makes **12**
Preparation time **15 minutes**,
  plus cooling
Cooking time **25 minutes**

2 **corn on the cobs**
4 **smoked streaky bacon
  rashers**, finely chopped
1 small **onion**, finely chopped
275 g (9 oz) **cornmeal**
1 tablespoon **baking powder**
½ teaspoon **salt**
1½ teaspoons **crushed
  dried chillies**
1 teaspoon **cumin seeds**,
  crushed
4 tablespoons **fresh
  coriander**, chopped
2 **eggs**
65 g (2½ oz) **lightly salted
  butter**, melted
225 ml (7½ fl oz) **milk**

Line a 12-section muffin tray with paper muffin cases.
Cook the corn cobs in a large saucepan of boiling
water for 5 minutes. Drain and leave to cool. Using a
knife, strip the kernels away from the cobs.

Put the bacon and onion in a small, dry frying pan and
cook gently, stirring frequently, until the bacon is turning
crisp and golden. Leave to cool.

Mix together the cornmeal, baking powder, salt, chillies,
cumin and coriander in a bowl. Stir in the bacon, onion
and corn.

Beat the eggs with the melted butter and milk and add
to the dry ingredients. Use a large metal spoon to stir
the ingredients gently together until only just combined.
Divide the muffin mixture between the paper cases.

Bake in a preheated oven, 220°C (425°F), Gas Mark 7,
for 15 minutes or until risen and pale golden. Serve
warm or cold.

For Indian spiced cornbreads, crush 12 cardamom
pods in a mortar with a pestle. Remove and discard
the shells and add 1 teaspoon each of coriander and
fennel seeds. Grind with the cardamom seeds. Make
the muffin mixture as above, but omit the corn and fry
the seeds in 1 tablespoon vegetable oil with the onion
and 2 finely chopped celery sticks instead of the
bacon. Bake as above.

red pepper & pine nut cupcakes

Makes **12**

Preparation time **20 minutes**, plus cooling

Cooking time **30 minutes**

150 g (5 oz) **lightly salted butter**, softened

2 **red peppers**, cored, deseeded and diced

2 **shallots**, thinly sliced

2 **garlic cloves**, crushed

75 g (3 oz) **pine nuts**

125 g (4 oz) **plain flour**

2 teaspoons **baking powder**

125 g (4 oz) **ground almonds**

4 **eggs**, beaten

12 small **bay leaves** (optional)

pepper

Line a 12-section bun tray with paper cake cases. Melt 25 g (1 oz) of the butter in a frying pan and gently fry the red peppers, shallots and garlic for 5 minutes until soft. Drain to a plate. Tip the pine nuts into the pan and cook for 2–3 minutes until beginning to brown. Leave to cool.

Put the remaining butter in a bowl with the flour, baking powder, ground almonds, eggs and plenty of pepper. Stir well to mix, then stir in the red pepper mixture and pine nuts. Divide the cake mixture between the paper cases and push a bay leaf into the top of each cake, if liked.

Bake in a preheated oven, 180°C (350°F), Gas Mark 4, for 20 minutes or until risen and just firm. Transfer to a wire rack. Serve warm or cold.

For artichoke & caper cupcakes, thoroughly drain a 275 g (9 oz) jar artichoke antipasta and cut the artichokes into small pieces. Rinse and drain 2 tablespoons capers. Make the cake mixture as above, but omit the peppers, shallots and garlic, reduce the butter to 125 g (4 oz) and add the artichokes and capers in place of the red pepper mixture with the pine nuts. Bake as above.

goats' cheese & tomato cakes

Makes **12**
Preparation time **25 minutes**
Cooking time **15 minutes**

325 g (11 oz) **plain flour**, plus
    extra for dusting
1 tablespoon **baking powder**
½ teaspoon **salt**
½ teaspoon **dried oregano**
8 g (¼ oz) **basil**, torn into
    small pieces
2 **spring onions**, finely
    chopped
100 g (3½ oz) **sun-blush
    tomatoes**, drained and
    chopped
284 ml (9½ fl oz) carton
    buttermilk
1 **egg yolk**
200 g (7 oz) **goats' cheese**,
    cut into small pieces
milk, for glazing
pepper

Cut out 12 x 13 cm (5 inch) squares of nonstick baking parchment and press a square into each section of a 12-section muffin tray. Mix together the flour, baking powder, salt and oregano in a bowl. Stir in the basil, spring onions and tomatoes.

Mix the buttermilk with the egg yolk, add to the bowl and stir until only just combined, sprinkling in a little more flour if the mixture is very sticky.

Turn out on to a lightly floured work surface and cut into 12 even-sized pieces. Shape each into a ball. Drop one ball into each of the lined tin sections.

Push your thumb into each ball to create a small cavity in the centre and insert a few pieces of goats' cheese into each. Brush with milk to glaze. Sprinkle with plenty of pepper.

Bake in a preheated oven, 220°C (425°F), Gas Mark 7, for 15 minutes or until risen and beginning to colour. Transfer to a wire rack to cool.

For leek & Gruyère cupcakes, roughly chop 1 leek and fry gently in 25 g (1 oz) lightly salted butter until softened. Mix together the dry ingredients as above, but then add the leek, 75 g (3 oz) grated Gruyère cheese and ½ teaspoon freshly grated nutmeg instead of the basil, spring onions and tomatoes. Mix in the wet ingredients and shape into balls as above, but omit the goats' cheese. Brush with milk to glaze, season with plenty of pepper and bake as above.

parmesan & pancetta cupcakes

Makes **9**

Preparation time **20 minutes**, plus cooling

Cooking time **25–30 minutes**

100 g (3½ oz) **thinly sliced pancetta**

5 tablespoons **olive oil**

300 g (10 oz) **self-raising flour**

2 teaspoons **baking powder**

50 g (2 oz) **Parmesan cheese**, finely grated

200 ml (7 fl oz) **milk**

1 **egg**, beaten

2 tablespoons **grainy mustard**

Line 9 sections of a 12-section muffin tray with paper muffin cases. Cut 9 x 5 cm (2 inch) strips from the pancetta. Finely chop the remainder. Heat 1 tablespoon of the oil in a small frying pan and gently fry the pancetta strips for 5 minutes until turning crisp. Drain to a plate. Fry the chopped pancetta in the pan for 3–4 minutes. Leave to cool.

Put the flour and baking powder in a bowl. Stir in the Parmesan and chopped pancetta until evenly mixed.

Whisk together the remaining oil, milk, egg and mustard with a fork in a jug and add to the bowl. Stir gently until only just combined.

Divide the muffin mixture between the paper cases and place a strip of pancetta on top of each.

Bake in a preheated oven, 200°C (400°F), Gas Mark 6, for 15–20 minutes or until risen and pale golden. Transfer to a wire rack. Serve warm or cold.

For chorizo & rosemary cupcakes, cut a 100 g (3½ oz) piece of chorizo sausage into small dice. Fry the chorizo instead of the pancetta strips in the oil as above. Add to the flour and baking powder with the Parmesan, then continue to make the mixture as above, but whisk 2 teaspoons finely chopped rosemary in with the oil, milk and egg (omit the mustard). Spoon into the paper cases and top each with a rosemary sprig before baking.

smoked salmon cakes

Makes **18**

Preparation time **25 minutes**, plus cooling

Cooking time **10 minutes**

150 g (5 oz) **buckwheat flour**

50 g (2 oz) **self-raising flour**

½ teaspoon **baking powder**

3 tablespoons chopped **dill**, plus extra sprigs to garnish

2 tablespoons chopped **parsley**

good pinch of **salt**

50 g (2 oz) **lightly salted butter**, melted

150 ml (¼ pint) **milk**, plus 2 tablespoons

2 **eggs**, beaten

300 g (10 oz) **cream cheese**

100 g (3½ oz) **smoked salmon**

pepper

Line 18 sections of 2 x 12-section bun trays with paper cake cases. Put the flours, baking powder, dill, parsley and salt in a bowl and mix together.

Whisk together the melted butter, the 150 ml (¼ pint) milk and the eggs with a fork in a jug and pour into the bowl. Using a large metal spoon, gently mix the ingredients together until evenly combined. Divide the mixture between the paper cases so that they are about half full.

Bake in a preheated oven, 200°C (400°F), Gas Mark 6, for 10 minutes or until slightly risen and firm to the touch. Transfer to a wire rack to cool, peeling away the paper cases, if liked.

Beat the cream cheese in a bowl to soften, then beat in the remaining milk. Pipe or spread the mixture over the cakes. Cut the salmon into strips and roll up loosely to resemble flowers. Use to decorate the tops of the cakes. Garnish with dill sprigs and a grinding of pepper.

For malted pepper & herb muffins, rinse and drain 2 tablespoons green peppercorns in brine and lightly crush. Line 8 sections of a 12-section muffin tray with paper muffin cases. Make the mixture as above, but use 150 g (5 oz) malt flour instead of the buckwheat flour and the peppercorns in place of the dill. Bake as above. Beat 150 g (5 oz) cream cheese with 1 tablespoon rinsed, drained and chopped capers, 4 chopped small gherkins and 1 tablespoon chopped parsley. Serve with the muffins.

spicy cheese & parsnip muffins

Makes **10**
Preparation time **20 minutes**,
  plus cooling
Cooking time **30 minutes**

250 g (8 oz) **parsnips**, diced
approximately 225 ml
  (7 fl oz) **milk**
4 tablespoons **olive oil**
1 **egg**, beaten
1 teaspoon **Tabasco sauce**
2 teaspoons **pink**
  peppercorns, crushed
275 g (9 oz) **plain flour**
1 tablespoon **baking powder**
75 g (3 oz) **Gruyère cheese**,
  finely grated
salt

Line 10 sections of a 12-section muffin tray with paper muffin cases. Cook the parsnips in a saucepan of lightly salted boiling water for 10 minutes until tender. Drain, mash and leave to cool.

Beat the milk into the cooled parsnips along with the oil, egg, Tabasco sauce and 1 teaspoon of the peppercorns, adding a dash more milk if the mixture feels dry.

Put the flour, baking powder, ½ teaspoon salt and all but 1 tablespoon of the cheese in a large bowl and mix well. Add the parsnip mixture and stir with a large metal spoon until the ingredients are only just combined.

Divide the muffin mixture between the paper cases and sprinkle with the remaining cheese, peppercorns and a little extra salt.

Bake in a preheated oven, 220°C (425°F), Gas Mark 7, for 20 minutes or until risen and pale golden. Transfer to a wire rack. Serve warm or cold.

For celeriac & mushroom muffins, cook 250 g (8 oz) diced celeriac in a saucepan of boiling water until just tender. Drain and mash well. Thinly slice 200 g (7 oz) small mushrooms and fry in 25 g (1 oz) butter until all the moisture has evaporated. Leave to cool. Make the muffin mixture as above, but use the celeriac mash instead of the parsnip mash and 1 teaspoon crushed green peppercorns instead of pink peppercorns, then stir the mushrooms into the dry ingredients. Once divided between the paper cases as above, sprinkle with another teaspoon crushed green peppercorns along with the remaining cheese and a little extra salt as above. Bake as above.

pumpkin & red onion cupcakes

Makes **12**

Preparation time **25 minutes**, plus cooling

Cooking time **50 minutes– 1 hour**

550 g (1 lb 2 oz) **pumpkin** or **butternut squash**

1 **red onion**, sliced

5 tablespoons **olive oil**

275 g (9 oz) **self-raising flour**

50 g (2 oz) **cornmeal**

15 g (½ oz) chopped **fresh coriander**

½ teaspoon **celery salt**

2 teaspoons **baking powder**

3 **eggs**, beaten

150 ml (¼ pint) **milk**

Line a 12-section muffin tray with paper muffin cases. Cut the pumpkin or squash into small dice, discarding the skin and seeds – you should have about 350 g (11½ oz) flesh. Spread out in a roasting tin with the onion slices and drizzle with 1 tablespoon of the oil. Roast in a preheated oven, 220°C (425°F), Gas Mark 7, for 30–40 minutes, turning once or twice, until beginning to colour. Leave to cool.

Mix together the flour, cornmeal, coriander, celery salt and baking powder in a bowl. Whisk together the eggs, milk and remaining oil with a fork in a jug.

Stir the cooled pumpkin or squash and onion into the dry ingredients. Add the egg mixture and mix together until the ingredients are only just combined. Divide the muffin mixture between the paper cases.

Bake in the oven for 20 minutes or until risen and just firm. Transfer to a wire rack to cool. Serve warm or cold.

For lentil cakes with crushed spices, thoroughly drain a 400 g (13 oz) can green lentils. Crush 1 teaspoon each of coriander, fennel and cumin seeds in a mortar with a pestle. Make the muffin mixture as above, but use the lentils in place of the roasted vegetables, whisk 1 teaspoon medium curry paste into the egg mixture and add the spices with the dry ingredients. Bake as above.

mini cheese & chive cakes

Makes **20**
Preparation time **10 minutes**
Cooking time **10–12 minutes**

200 g (7 oz) **self-raising flour**
1 teaspoon **baking powder**
good pinch of **salt**
50 g (2 oz) **mature Cheddar cheese**, finely grated
4 tablespoons snipped **chives**
50 g (2 oz) **lightly salted butter**, melted
7 tablespoons **milk**
1 **egg**, beaten

Line 20 sections of 2 x 12-section mini muffin trays with mini paper cake cases. Put the flour, baking powder and salt in a bowl. Stir in the cheese and chives until evenly mixed.

Whisk together the melted butter, milk and egg with a fork in a jug and add to the bowl. Stir well to form a thick paste. Divide the mixture between the paper cases.

Bake in a preheated oven, 200°C (400°F), Gas Mark 6, for 10–12 minutes or until risen and pale golden. Transfer to a wire rack. Serve warm or cold.

For mini Parmesan & olive cakes, chop 50 g (2 oz) pitted black olives into small pieces and mix with the dry ingredients as above, but use 50 g (2 oz) finely grated Parmesan cheese instead of the Cheddar and omit the chives. Continue making the mixture as above, but whisk 1 tablespoon tapenade in with the melted butter, milk and egg. Bake as above.

rye & caraway buns

Makes **12**
Preparation time **10 minutes**
Cooking time **20 minutes**

3 tablespoons **black treacle**
50 g (2 oz) **lightly salted butter**, plus extra for greasing
1 **egg**
225 ml (7½ fl oz) **milk**
150 g (5 oz) **rye flour**
150 g (5 oz) **plain flour**
1 tablespoon **baking powder**
½ teaspoon **salt**
2 teaspoons **caraway seeds**

Grease a 12-section muffin tray, preferably nonstick. Put the treacle and butter in a small saucepan and heat gently until the butter has melted. Whisk together the egg and milk with a fork in a jug and stir in the treacle and butter.

Put the flours, baking powder, salt and caraway seeds in a bowl and add the wet ingredients. Stir gently until the ingredients are evenly combined. Divide the mixture between the tin sections.

Bake in a preheated oven, 220°C (425°F), Gas Mark 7, for 15 minutes or until well risen. Transfer to a wire rack. Serve warm or cold.

For easy Boston buns, make the mixture as above, but replace 75 g (3 oz) of the plain flour with 50 g (2 oz) wholemeal flour and 25 g (1 oz) cornmeal, omit the caraway seeds and add 50 g (2 oz) raisins to the dry ingredients. Bake as above.

saffron & potato buns

Makes **12**
Preparation time **20 minutes**, plus cooling
Cooking time **25 minutes**

300 g (10 oz) **potatoes**, diced
½ teaspoon crumbled **saffron strands**
1 tablespoon **boiling water**
200 ml (7 fl oz) **milk**
4 tablespoons **olive oil**
1 **egg**, beaten
275 g (9 oz) **plain flour**
1 tablespoon **baking powder**
2 teaspoons chopped **thyme**, plus extra sprigs for sprinkling
1 teaspoon **sea salt**, plus extra for sprinkling
egg yolk lightly whisked with 1 teaspoon **water**, for glazing
butter, to serve

Line a 12-section bun tray with paper cake cases. Cook the potatoes in a saucepan of salted boiling water for 8 minutes or until only just tender. Drain and leave to cool.

Mix the saffron with the boiling water in a jug and leave to stand for 5 minutes. Whisk together the saffron and water, milk, oil and egg with a fork in a bowl.

Mix together the flour, baking powder, chopped thyme and salt in a separate bowl, then stir in the potato. Add the saffron mixture and mix with a large metal spoon until evenly combined.

Divide the mixture between the paper cases. Brush the tops lightly with the egg yolk mixture. Sprinkle with a little extra salt and scatter with thyme sprigs. Bake in a preheated oven, 220°C (425°F), Gas Mark 7, for 15 minutes or until risen and pale golden. Transfer to a wire rack. Serve warm or cold, split and buttered.

For carrot & coriander buns, dice 275 g (9 oz) carrots and cook in a saucepan of lightly salted boiling water until just tender. Drain thoroughly. Whisk together the milk, oil and egg as above, omitting the saffron and water, and add 1 teaspoon medium curry paste. Continue to make the mixture as above, but use 2 tablespoons chopped fresh coriander in place of the thyme and stir in the cooked carrots instead of the potato. Once divided between the paper cases, brush the tops with the egg yolk mixture, sprinkle with a little extra salt and bake as above.

special occasion cupcakes

christmas garland

Makes **1 garland of 24 cupcakes**
Preparation time **25 minutes**, plus cooling
Cooking time **20–25 minutes**

6 tablespoons **apricot jam**
1 tablespoon **water**
24 **Cranberry Spice Cupcakes** (see page 22) or **Fruit & Nut Cupcakes** (see page 24)
icing sugar, for dusting
bunch of **red seedless grapes**
bunch of **green seedless grapes**
3–4 **clementines**, halved
3–4 **dried whole figs**, halved
plenty of **bay leaf sprigs**

Press the jam through a sieve into a small saucepan and add the water. Heat gently until softened, then spread in a thin layer over the tops of the cooled cakes.

Arrange 15–16 of the cakes in a staggered circle on a round flat platter or tray, at least 35 cm (14 inches) in diameter. Using a small, fine sieve or tea strainer, dust the cakes on the platter with plenty of icing sugar.

Fold a piece of paper into 4 thicknesses, then cut out a holly leaf shape, about 6 cm (2½ inches) long. Press a holly leaf paper template gently on to the centre of 4 more cakes and dust lavishly with icing sugar. Carefully lift off the templates by sliding a knife under the paper to remove them without disturbing the sugar. Repeat on the remaining cakes. Arrange the cakes in a circle on top of the first layer.

Cut the grapes into small clusters. Tuck all the fruits into the gaps around the cakes and into the centre of the plate. Finish by arranging small sprigs of bay leaves around the fruits.

For cranberry glazed cupcakes, put 150 g (5 oz) fresh cranberries in a small saucepan with 50 g (2 oz) caster sugar, ½ teaspoon ground ginger, 2 tablespoons port and 1 tablespoon water. Heat gently until the sugar has dissolved, then simmer until the cranberries are soft and beginning to split. Tip into a bowl and leave to cool. Beat 250 g (8 oz) mascarpone cheese with 5 tablespoons icing sugar and pipe a little around the edges of the cooled cakes. Pile the cranberry mixture into the centres.

mincemeat cupcakes

Makes **12**
Preparation time **20 minutes**,
  plus cooling
Cooking time **20–25 minutes**

125 g (4 oz) **lightly salted
  butter**, softened
25 g (1 oz) **dark
  muscovado sugar**
2 **eggs**
150 g (5 oz) **self-raising flour**
½ teaspoon **baking powder**
1 teaspoon **ground mixed
  spice**
1 tablespoon **milk**
300 g (10 oz) **luxury
  mincemeat**

Topping
300 ml (½ pint) **double cream**
4 tablespoons **sherry**
2 tablespoons **icing sugar**
edible pink and silver balls,
  to decorate

Line a 12-section muffin tray with silver or gold foil muffin cases. Put the butter, muscovado sugar, eggs, flour, baking powder, mixed spice and milk in a bowl and beat with a hand-held electric whisk for about a minute until light and creamy. Add the mincemeat and stir in until evenly mixed. Divide the cake mixture between the foil cases.

Bake in a preheated oven, 180°C (350°F), Gas Mark 4, for 20–25 minutes or until risen and just firm to the touch. Transfer to a wire rack to cool.

Put the cream, sherry and icing sugar in a bowl and whip until the mixture only just holds its shape. Pile the cream over the cakes and scatter with pink and silver balls to decorate.

For Christmas pudding cupcakes, roll out 50 g (2 oz) green ready-to-roll icing thinly on a work surface lightly dusted with icing sugar and cut out 24 small holly shapes using a cutter. Roll 36 tiny holly berries from a small piece of red ready-to-roll icing. Transfer to a sheet of greaseproof and leave to harden. Make and bake the cakes as above. Blend 2 tablespoons smooth apricot jam with 2 teaspoons sherry and brush over the tops of the cooled cakes. Roll out 100 g (3½ oz) white ready-to-roll icing thinly and cut out small rounds with a slightly wavy edge. Arrange on top of the cakes and decorate with the leaves and berries, securing with a dampened paintbrush.

christmas stars

Makes **12**

Preparation time **35 minutes**, plus cooling

Cooking time **20 minutes**

100 g (3½ oz) **white ready-to-roll icing**

12 **Vanilla Cupcakes** (see page 22)

½ quantity **Buttercream** (see page 18)

200 g (7 oz) **icing sugar**, plus extra for dusting

4–5 teaspoons **water**

25 g (1 oz) **desiccated coconut**

Knead the white ready-to-roll icing on a work surface lightly dusted with icing sugar. Roll out thickly and cut out small star shapes using a cutter. Transfer to a baking sheet lined with nonstick baking parchment and leave to harden while decorating the cakes.

Cut out a deep, cone-shaped centre from each cooled cake using a small, sharp knife. Fill each cavity with buttercream and position a cut-out cone on each with the crust side face down.

Mix the icing sugar with the water in a bowl until smooth – the icing should hold its shape but not be too firm. Carefully spread the icing over the tops of the cakes and scatter with desiccated coconut.

Gently press a star into the top of each cake and leave to set.

For winter wonderland cakes, roll out 150 g (5 oz) white ready-to-roll icing on a work surface lightly dusted with icing sugar and cut out Christmas tree shapes using small cutters in 2 or 3 different sizes – you need 24 altogether. Transfer to a tray lined with nonstick baking parchment and leave to harden for several hours or overnight. Make and bake the cakes as above. Beat together 75 g (3 oz) softened unsalted butter and 125 g (4 oz) icing sugar until smooth and spread over the cooled cakes. Press the trees gently down into the buttercream. Serve dusted with icing sugar.

snow-covered ginger buns

Makes **12**

Preparation time **30 minutes**, plus cooling & setting

Cooking time **15–20 minutes**

125 g (4 oz) **lightly salted butter**

125 ml (4 fl oz) **maple syrup**

125 g (4 oz) **light muscovado sugar**

225 g (7½ oz) **self-raising flour**

1 teaspoon **baking powder**

1 teaspoon **ground ginger**

2 **eggs**

125 ml (4 fl oz) **milk**

3 tablespoons **glacé ginger**, chopped, plus extra to decorate

Icing

200 g (7 oz) **icing sugar**, sifted

4 teaspoons **water**

2 pieces of **glacé ginger**, sliced

Line a 12-section bun tray with paper or foil cake cases. Put the butter, maple syrup and muscovado sugar in a saucepan and heat gently, stirring, until the butter has melted. Mix together the flour, baking powder and ground ginger in a bowl. Beat together the eggs and milk in a separate bowl.

Take the butter pan off the heat, then beat in the flour mixture. Gradually beat in the egg and milk mixture, then stir in the glacé ginger. Divide the cake mixture between the cake cases.

Bake in a preheated oven, 180°C (350°F), Gas Mark 4, for 10–15 minutes or until well risen and cracked. Transfer to a wire rack to cool.

Sift the icing sugar into a bowl and gradually mix in the water to create a smooth, spoonable icing. Drizzle random lines of icing from a spoon over the muffins and decorate with slices of glacé ginger. Leave to harden for 30 minutes before serving.

For jewelled Christmas muffins, make the cake mixture as above, but use 6 finely chopped glacé cherries instead of the glacé ginger. Mix together 100 g (3½ oz) chopped multicoloured glacé cherries and 25 g (1 oz) chopped semi-dried pineapple. Make the icing as above, spread over the cooled cakes and scatter with the glacé fruit mixture and plenty of edible gold or silver balls.

easter nests

Makes **12**

Preparation time **35 minutes**,
  plus cooling

Cooking time **25 minutes**

1 quantity **Chocolate Fudge
  Frosting** (see page 18)

12 **Chocolate Cupcakes**
  (see page 22)

200 g (7 oz) **flaked chocolate
  bars**, cut into 2.5 cm
  (1 inch) lengths

36 **candy-covered chocolate
  mini eggs**

Spread the chocolate frosting over the tops of the cooled cakes using a small palette knife, spreading it right to the edges.

Cut the short lengths of flaked chocolate bars lengthways into thin 'shards'.

Arrange the chocolate shards around the edges of the cakes, pressing them into the icing at different angles to resemble birds' nests. Pile 3 eggs into the centre of each 'nest'.

For chocolate chestnut cupcakes, make and bake the cakes as on page 22, but add ½ teaspoon ground cinnamon with the cocoa powder to the cake mixture. Pierce the tops of the cooled cakes with a skewer and drizzle each with 1 tablespoon brandy. Beat together 200 g (7 oz) chestnut purée and 2 tablespoons brandy. Whip 300 ml (½ pint) double cream with 25 g (1 oz) icing sugar until just peaking. Stir in the chestnut purée and pile on top of the cakes. Sprinkle with chocolate curls.

easter cupcakes

Makes **12**

Preparation time **30 minutes**, plus cooling

Cooking time **20 minutes**

125 g (4 oz) **lightly salted butter**, softened

125 g (4 oz) **caster sugar**

2 **eggs**

100 g (3½ oz) **self-raising flour**

½ teaspoon **baking powder**

50 g (2 oz) **ground almonds**

finely grated **rind** of 1 **lemon**

Icing

75 g (3 oz) **unsalted butter**, softened

150 g (5 oz) **icing sugar**

1 teaspoon **vanilla extract**

125 g (4 oz) **fondant icing sugar**

3–4 tablespoons **lemon juice**

a few drops of **yellow food colouring**

12 **sugar flowers**, to decorate

Line a 12-section bun tray with paper cake cases. Put all the cake ingredients in a bowl and beat with a hand-held electric whisk for 1–2 minutes until light and creamy. Divide the cake mixture between the paper cases.

Bake in a preheated oven, 180°C (350°F), Gas Mark 4, for 20 minutes or until risen and just firm to the touch. Transfer to a wire rack to cool.

Beat together the unsalted butter, icing sugar and vanilla extract in a bowl until smooth. Place a teaspoonful on top of each cake and mould into a smooth dome using a knife.

Beat the fondant icing sugar with enough lemon juice in a separate bowl to make an icing that doesn't quite hold its shape. Beat in the food colouring. Place a teaspoonful on top of the buttercream. Ease the icing over the tops of the cakes to cover the buttercream completely. Decorate each cake with a sugar flower.

For festive spice cupcakes, make the cake mixture as above, but use the grated rind of 1 orange and 1 teaspoon ground mixed spice instead of the grated lemon rind. Bake as above. Make the fondant icing as above, but use 2–3 tablespoons orange juice in place of the lemon juice and colour the icing with a few drops of red food colouring. Spread the icing over the cooled cakes and decorate with whole spices such as star anise, pieces of cinnamon stick, cardamom pods and whole cloves.

mini simnel cakes

Makes **12**

Preparation time **30 minutes**, plus cooling & soaking

Cooking time **30 minutes**

125 g (4 oz) **lightly salted butter**, softened, plus extra for greasing

50 g (2 oz) **light muscovado sugar**

1 piece of **stem ginger** from a jar, finely chopped, plus 2 tablespoons **ginger syrup**

2 **eggs**

150 g (5 oz) **self-raising flour**

½ teaspoon **baking powder**

½ teaspoon freshly grated **nutmeg**

200 g (7 oz) **luxury mixed dried fruit**, soaked in 3 tablespoons **brandy** or **orange-flavoured liqueur** for 1 hour

325 g (11 oz) **white almond paste**

icing sugar, for dusting

Line a 12-section bun tray with paper cases. Put the butter, sugar, ginger, eggs, flour, baking powder and nutmeg in a bowl and beat with a hand-held electric whisk for about a minute until smooth and creamy. Stir in the fruit and any liquid until evenly mixed.

Roll 100 g (3½ oz) of the almond paste into a log shape, about 6 cm (2½ inches) long, and cut into 12 slices. Divide half the cake mixture between the cases and level with the back of a teaspoon. Place a paste slice over each. Cover with the remaining mixture.

Bake in a preheated oven, 180°C (350°F), Gas Mark 4, for about 25 minutes until just firm to the touch. Transfer to a wire rack to cool.

Roll out the remaining paste thinly on a work surface lightly dusted with icing sugar. Cut out 12 rounds with a 5 cm (2 inch) cookie cutter. Brush the cakes with the ginger syrup and cover each with a paste round. Flatten a small piece of paste into a thin ribbon and roll up to make a rose. Position on the cake centre. Repeat for the remaining cakes. Put on a baking sheet and heat under a moderate grill, watching closely, until lightly toasted.

For citrus simnel cakes, beat together 125 g (4 oz) softened lightly salted butter, 75 g (3 oz) caster sugar, 2 eggs, 100 g (3½ oz) self-raising flour, ½ teaspoon baking powder, 50 g (2 oz) ground almonds and the finely grated rind of 1 orange and 1 lemon. Scatter with 200 g (7 oz) diced almond paste before baking as above. Mix 50 g (2 oz) icing sugar with 1–1½ teaspoons lemon juice and drizzle over the cooled cakes.

flying bats

Makes **12**

Preparation time **40 minutes**, plus cooling & setting

Cooking time **20 minutes**

125 g (4 oz) **black ready-to-roll icing**

icing sugar, for dusting

2 tablespoons **clear honey**

12 **Vanilla Cupcakes** (see page 22)

175 g (6 oz) **orange ready-to-roll icing**

1 tube of **black writing icing**

selection of tiny **red**, **orange** and **yellow sweets**

Knead the black ready-to roll icing on a work surface lightly dusted with icing sugar. Roll out thickly and cut out 12 small bat shapes by hand or using a cutter. Transfer to a baking sheet lined with nonstick baking parchment and leave to harden while decorating the cakes.

Spread ½ teaspoon of the honey over the top of each cooled cake. Roll out the orange icing thinly and cut out 12 rounds using a 6 cm (2½ inch) cookie cutter. Place an orange round on top of each cake.

Place a bat on top of each cake. Dampen the edge of the orange icing and pipe a wiggly line of black icing around the edge. Press the sweets gently into the icing, over the black wiggly line.

For spooky spider cakes, spread each cake with a thin layer of apricot or red fruit jam. Roll out 200 g (7 oz) green or blue ready-to-roll icing thinly on a work surface lightly dusted with icing sugar and cut out 12 rounds using a 6 cm (2½ inch) cookie cutter. Position one on each cake. Using a tube of black writing icing, pipe small spiders' webs on to each cake. Decorate with jelly 'bug' sweets.

stars, spots & stripes

Makes **12**
Preparation time **40 minutes**, plus cooling
Cooking time **20 minutes**

½ quantity **Buttercream** (see page 18)
12 **Vanilla Cupcakes** (see page 22)
150 g (5 oz) **white ready-to-roll icing**
125 g (4 oz) **blue ready-to-roll icing**
icing sugar, for dusting

Spread the buttercream in a thin layer over the tops of the cooled cakes using a small palette knife.

Knead the icings on a work surface lightly dusted with icing sugar. Take 50 g (2 oz) of the white icing, roll out thinly and cut out 4 rounds using a 6 cm (2½ inch) cookie cutter. Cut out 6 small stars from each round using a cutter. Roll out a little of the blue icing thinly and cut out 24 stars. Fit the blue stars into each white round and transfer to 4 of the cakes.

Roll out another 50 g (2 oz) of the white icing thinly. Roll tiny balls of blue icing between your finger and thumb. Press at intervals on to the white icing. Gently roll with a rolling pin so that the blue icing forms dots. Cut out 4 rounds and transfer to 4 more cakes.

Cut long strips 5 mm (¼ inch) wide from the remaining blue and white icing and lay them together on the work surface. Roll lightly with a rolling pin to flatten and secure them together, then cut out 4 more rounds. Place on top of the remaining 4 cakes.

For star & moon cupcakes, make and bake 12 Chocolate Cupcakes (see page 22). Melt 100 g (3½ oz) white chocolate (see pages 16–17). Draw 6 star and 6 moon shapes on to nonstick baking parchment using 5–6cm (2–2½ inch) cutters as guides. Put the chocolate into a paper piping bag (see page 15) and use to fill the shapes. Leave to set. Melt 100 g (3½ oz) plain chocolate with 15 g (½ oz) unsalted butter and spread over the cakes. Peel the paper away from the shapes and position on the cakes.

firework sparklers

Makes **12**

Preparation time **40 minutes**, plus cooling & setting

Cooking time **25–30 minutes**

100 g (3½ oz) **butternut squash**, peeled and deseeded

125 g (4 oz) **lightly salted butter**, softened

50 g (2 oz) **light muscovado sugar**

100 g (3½ oz) **clear honey**

2 **eggs**

150 g (5 oz) **self-raising flour**

50 g (2 oz) **porridge oats**

½ teaspoon **baking powder**

1 teaspoon **ground mixed spice**

To decorate

50 g (2 oz) **orange ready-to-roll icing**

50 g (2 oz) **white ready-to-roll icing**

200 g (7 oz) **fondant icing sugar**, plus extra for dusting

2 tablespoons **orange juice**

4 tablespoons **orange curd**

indoor sparklers

Line a 12-section bun tin with paper or foil cake cases. Grate the squash into a bowl and add all the remaining cake ingredients. Beat with a hand-held electric whisk for about a minute until light and creamy. Divide the cake mixture between the paper or foil cases.

Bake in a preheated oven, 180°C (350°F), Gas Mark 4, for 25–30 minutes or until just firm to the touch. Transfer to a wire rack to cool.

Roll out the orange and white icing on a work surface lightly dusted with icing sugar and cut out small star shapes, either by hand or using a cutter. Push a wooden cocktail stick into each and place on a sheet of greaseproof paper to harden for at least an hour.

Beat the fondant icing sugar in a bowl with 2 tablespoons orange juice, adding a little extra juice if necessary to give a thick but spreadable consistency. Spoon over the cakes, spreading to the edges. Take a teaspoon of the orange curd and pour it, in a loose spiral, over each cake. Push an icing star down into each cake. Just before serving, position the sparklers on the cakes and light.

For honey-drizzled spice cakes, make the cake mixture as above, but use 2 teaspoons ground mixed spice and add ½ teaspoon ground cinnamon. Bake as above and leave to cool. Beat 200 g (7 oz) Greek yogurt with 1 tablespoon clear honey and spread over the cakes. Drizzle with extra honey to decorate.

wedding cupcakes

Makes **12**
Preparation time **30 minutes**,
  plus cooling
Cooking time **20 minutes**

12 **Vanilla Cupcakes**
  (see page 22)
4 tablespoons **sherry** or
  orange-flavoured liqueur
  (optional)
200 g (7 oz) **icing sugar**,
  sifted
1–2 tablespoons **lemon juice**
36 **sugared almonds**
12 **frosted flowers**
  (see page 228)
fine white ribbon, to decorate

Drizzle the cakes with the sherry or liqueur, if using. Mix the icing sugar with 1 tablespoon of the lemon juice in a bowl. Slowly add the remaining lemon juice, stirring well with a wooden spoon, until the icing holds its shape but is not difficult to spread – you may not need all the juice.

Spread the lemon-flavoured icing over the tops of the cooled cakes using a small palette knife and arrange 3 sugared almonds in the centre of each.

Place a frosted flower on top of each cake and tie a length of white ribbon around each paper cake case to decorate it, finishing it with a bow.

For big birthday cupcakes, roll out 100 g (3½ oz) ready-to-roll icing in the colour of your choice and stamp out appropriate numbers using cutters. Transfer to a tray lined with nonstick baking parchment and leave to harden for several hours or overnight. Make and bake the Vanilla Cupcakes as on page 22, but substitute 50 g (2 oz) grated white chocolate for 50 g (2 oz) of the caster sugar in the cake ingredients. Melt 100 g (3½ oz) chopped white chocolate with 65 g (2½ oz) unsalted butter and 2 tablespoons milk in a saucepan, stirring until smooth. Turn into a bowl, beat in 100 g (3½ oz) icing sugar and continue beating with a wooden spoon until softly peaking. Spread over the cooled cakes, then gently arrange the icing numbers, vertically, on top of the cakes and scatter with sugar sprinkles.

valentine hearts

Makes **12**
Preparation time **30 minutes**,
  plus cooling
Cooking time **20 minutes**

200 g (7 oz) **icing sugar**,
  plus extra for dusting
4–5 teaspoons **rosewater**
  or **lemon juice**
12 **Vanilla Cupcakes**
  (see page 22)
100 g (3½ oz) **red**
  ready-to-roll icing
6 tablespoons **strawberry jam**

Put the icing sugar in a bowl and add 4 teaspoons of the rosewater or lemon juice. Mix until smooth, adding a little more liquid if necessary until the icing forms a thick paste. Spread over the tops of the cooled cakes.

Knead the red icing on a work surface lightly dusted with icing sugar. Roll out thickly and cut out 12 small heart shapes using a cutter. Place a heart on the top of each cake.

Press the jam through a small sieve to remove any lumps. Put the sieved jam in a small piping bag fitted with a writing nozzle. Pipe small dots into the icing around the edges of each cake and pipe a line of jam around the edge of each heart.

For frosted fruit & flower cakes, whip 150 ml (¼ pint) double cream with 3 tablespoons orange-flavoured liqueur in a small bowl and spread over the cooled cakes. Scatter with a selection of fresh raspberries, small red seedless grapes and fresh blueberries, and position a small red rose on top of each. Serve dusted with icing sugar.

frosted flower cupcakes

Makes **12**
Preparation time **40 minutes**,
  plus cooling & setting
Cooking time **20 minutes**

selection of small **edible**
  spring flowers, such as
  primroses, violets or rose
  petals, or **herb flowers**
1 **egg white**
caster sugar, for dusting
1 quantity **White Chocolate**
  Fudge Frosting
  (see page 18)
12 **Vanilla Cupcakes**
  (see page 22)
fine pastel-coloured ribbon,
  to decorate (optional)

Make sure the flowers are clean and thoroughly dry before frosting. Put the egg white in a small bowl and beat lightly with a fork. Put the sugar in a separate bowl.

Using your fingers or a soft paintbrush, coat all the petals on both sides with the egg white. Dust plenty of sugar over the flowers until evenly coated. Transfer to a sheet of nonstick baking parchment and leave for at least 1 hour until firm.

Spread the chocolate frosting over the tops of the cooled cakes using a small palette knife. Decorate the top of each with the frosted flowers. Tie a length of ribbon around each paper cake case to decorate, finishing it with a ribbon bow, if using.

For coconut frosted cakes, make and bake the Vanilla Cupcakes as on page 22, but add the finely grated rind of 2 limes and 1 tablespoon lime juice to the cake ingredients. Put 75 ml (3 fl oz) single cream in a saucepan with 50 g (2 oz) chopped creamed coconut. Heat gently until the coconut has melted. Turn into a bowl and add 2 teaspoons lime juice and 300 g (10 oz) icing sugar. Whisk until thick and smooth, then spread over the cooled cakes. Decorate with grated lime rind.

tee-off cakes

Makes **12**

Preparation time **40 minutes**,
plus cooling

Cooking time **20–25 minutes**

8 tablespons **chocolate
hazelnut spread** or
½ quantity **Chocolate Fudge
Frosting** (see page 18)
12 **Vanilla** or **Chocolate
Cupcakes** (see page 22)
200 g (7 oz) **green
ready-to-roll icing**
icing sugar, for dusting
75 g (3 oz) **white
ready-to-roll icing**
12 **foil-wrapped chocolate
golf balls**

Beat the chocolate spread or frosting to soften it slightly, then spread it over the tops of the cooled cakes using a small palette knife.

Knead the green icing on a work surface lightly dusted with icing sugar. Roll out thinly and cut out 12 rounds using a 5 cm (2 inch) cookie cutter. Place a green round on top of each cake.

Shape 12 small golf tees from the white ready-to-roll icing. Lay one on top of each cake, securing with a dampened paintbrush. Press a foil-wrapped chocolate golf ball into the icing, alongside the tee, to finish.

For football cupcakes, make the cakes as above and spread with chocolate fudge frosting. Beat 150g (5oz) fondant icing sugar in a bowl with a little green food colouring and enough cold water, about 3–4 teaspoons, for the icing to hold its shape but remain spreadable. Spoon a little icing over each cake and spread slightly to the edges so the chocolate icing still shows through. Position a foil-wrapped chocolate football on top of each cake.

daisy celebration cupcakes

Makes **24**

Preparation time **1–1½ hours**,
  plus cooling & setting

Cooking time **25 minutes**

250 g (8 oz) **lightly salted
  butter**, softened
250 g (8 oz) **caster sugar**
4 **eggs**
1 tablespoon **vanilla bean
  paste** or **vanilla extract**
finely grated **rind** of 2 **lemons**
300 g (10 oz) **self-raising
  flour**
1 teaspoon **baking powder**

To decorate
icing sugar, for dusting
125 g (4 oz) **pale pink
  ready-to-roll icing**
125 g (4 oz) **deep pink
  ready-to-roll icing**
300 ml (½ pint) **double
  cream**
300 g (10 oz) **white
  chocolate**, chopped into
  small dice

Line 2 x 12-section bun trays with paper cake cases.
Put all the cake ingredients in a bowl and beat with a
hand-held electric whisk for about a minute until light
and creamy. Divide the cake mixture between the
paper cases.

Bake in a preheated oven, 180°C (350°F), Gas Mark 4,
for 20 minutes or until just firm to the touch – the
cakes on the lower oven shelf may need a little longer,
but don't swap the trays halfway through cooking or
the cakes could sink. Transfer to a wire rack to cool.

Roll out the pale pink icing thinly on a work surface
lightly dusted with icing sugar. Stamp out 12 flower
shapes using a cutter about 4 cm (1¾ inches) in
diameter. Cup each flower slightly in the palm of your
hand and transfer to a sheet of crumpled foil to harden.
Roll out the deep pink icing and make 12 more flowers.
Take a tiny piece of pale pink icing from the trimmings
and press against a piece of tuille until the netting
leaves an impression in the icing. Peel away the tuille.
Press the icing gently into the centre of a deep pink
flower. Repeat for the remaining flowers, alternating
the pinks.

Put 200 ml (7 fl oz) of the cream in a small saucepan
and bring almost to the boil. Pour over the chocolate in
a bowl and leave until it has melted, stirring occasionally
until smooth. Leave to cool.

Stir the remaining cream into the chocolate mixture
and whip until just holding its shape – don't overwhip
or the mixture will start to separate. Pipe or spoon over
the cakes. Decorate with the prepared flowers.

index

A

almonds
   almond praline
      cupcakes 148
   breakfast fruit & nut
      cupcakes 66
   chocolate almond
      sandwich cakes 86
   citrus simnel cakes
      216
   Easter cupcakes
      214
   florentine cupcakes
      164
   frosted choc 'n' nut
      cupcakes 100
   liqueur-drizzled mocha
      cakes 178
   mini linzer cakes 154
   spiced sweet potato
      cupcakes 172
   sweet camomile
      muffins 162
alphabetti cupcakes
   108
amaretti biscuits, apricot
   & almond cupcakes
   174
apple & sultana muffins
   120
apricots
   apricot & almond
      cupcakes 174
   apricot & white
      chocolate cupcakes
      92
   frangipane & apricot
      cupcakes 154

spiced apricot &
   hazelnut cupcakes
   66
artichoke & caper
   cupcakes 184
autumn leaf cakes 136

B

bacon, corn, chilli &
   bacon muffins 182
bananas
   banoffi cream
      cupcakes 38
   frosted banana
      cupcakes 112
   honey & banana
      cakes 50
   yoghurt & banana
      cakes 50
banoffi cream cupcakes
   38
beetroot, red velvet
   cupcakes 166
big birthday cupcakes
   224
birthday cake stack 138
blueberries
   double berry muffins
      32
   frosted blueberry
      cupcakes 158
   white chocolate
      blueberry friands 96
Brazil nut & orange
   cupcakes 62
breakfast fruit & nut
   cupcakes 66

bun trays 11
busy bees 110
butter, creamy
   cinnamon 60
butter-iced ginger
   cupcakes 40
buttercream 18
   coffee 170
butterfly cupcakes 46
butternut squash,
   firework sparklers
   222

C

camomile, sweet
   camomile muffins
   162
capers, artichoke &
   caper cupcakes
   184
caramel sauce,
   homemade 36
caraway seeds, rye &
   caraway buns 198
cardamom,
   white-chocolate-
   frosted cardamom
   cakes 84
carrot & coriander buns
   200
cases, filling 13
celeriac & mushroom
   muffins 192
cheeky cats 124
cheese
   celeriac & mushroom
      muffins 192

chocolate ricotta
   cakes 98
fruity flower cupcakes
   132
goat's cheese &
   tomato cakes
   186
leek & Gruyère
   cupcakes 186
malted pepper & herb
   muffins 190
marsala raisin &
   ricotta cakes 144
mini cheese & chive
   cakes 196
mini Parmesan & olive
   cakes 196
Parmesan & pancetta
   cupcakes 188
raspberry amaretti
   cakes 174
red velvet cupcakes
   166
smoked salmon cakes
   190
spicy cheese &
   parsnip muffins
   192
spicy pear & goat's
   cheese cupcakes
   166
cheesecakes
   chocolate
      cheesecakes 74
   chocolate honeycomb
      cheesecakes 74
   rum & raisin
      cheesecakes 144

cherries
  florentine cupcakes 164
  reindeer cupcakes 130
  very cherry cupcakes 44
chestnuts, chocolate chestnut cupcakes 212
chillies, corn, chilli & bacon muffins 182
chives, mini cheese & chive cakes 196
chocolate 22, 68–103
  apricot & white chocolate cupcakes 92
  chocolate almond sandwich cakes 86
  chocolate blondie cupcakes 88
  chocolate cake stack 138
  chocolate cheesecakes 74
  chocolate chestnut cupcakes 212
  chocolate cream butterfly cupcakes 98
  chocolate crunchies 72
  chocolate fruit & nut cupcakes 72
  chocolate fudge cupcakes 70
  chocolate fudge frosting 18
  chocolate heart cakes 134

chocolate honeycomb cheesecakes 74
chocolate jaffa cupcakes 80
chocolate orange cupcakes 78
chocolate peanut cupcakes 80
chocolate prune cupcakes 78
chocolate raspberry friands 96
chocolate ricotta cakes 98
chocolate, rum & raisin cupcakes 94
chocolate snowball cupcakes 130
chocolate strawberry cupcakes 86
chocolate toffee cupcakes 90
dark chocolate & ginger muffins 102
Easter nests 212
florentine cupcakes 164
frosted choc 'n' nut cupcakes 100
melting 16
mini minted cupcakes 152
mint chocolate cupcakes 90
mocha cupcakes 94
reindeer cupcakes 130
rich fruit chocolate cupcakes 92
star & moon cupcakes 220

tee-off cakes 230
triple chocolate cupcakes 82
warm chocolate brownie cakes 88
wiggly worms 116
see also white chocolate
chorizo & rosemary cupcakes 188
Christmas garland 204
Christmas pudding cupcakes 206
Christmas stars 208
cinnamon, creamy cinnamon butter 60
citrus simnel cakes 216
clementines
  Christmas garland 204
  clementine cupcakes 112
coconut
  chocolate coconut kisses 76
  coconut frosted cakes 228
  piña colada cupcakes 150
  pineapple & coconut cupcakes 58
  pink coconut cupcakes 56
coffee
  buttercream 170
  coffee & walnut cupcakes 15, 170
  espresso cream cakes 178

liqueur-drizzled mocha cakes 178
marbled coffee cupcakes 28
mocha cupcakes 94
cooling the cakes 15
coriander, carrot & coriander buns 200
corn on the cob
  corn, chilli & bacon muffins 182
  Indian spiced cornbreads 182
courgette & hazelnut cupcakes 26
cranberries
  cranberry glazed cupcakes 204
  cranberry spice cupcakes 22, 204
cream
  chocolate cream butterfly cupcakes 98
  espresso cream cakes 178
  frosted fruit & flower cakes 226
  macadamia & raspberry cupcakes 160
  mincemeat cupcakes 206
  pistachio cream cupcakes 160
creamy cinnamon butter 60
crunchy peanut cupcakes 170
cutters 12

D

daisy celebration cupcakes 232
dark chocolate & ginger muffins 102
dates
  breakfast fruit & nut cupcakes 66
  chocolate fruit & nut cupcakes 72
  date & orange cupcakes 24
decorations, ready-made 17
double berry muffins 32
double chocolate whirls 82
ducks, bunnies & chicks 126

E

Easter chick & egg cakes 126
Easter cupcakes 214
Easter nests 212
easy Boston buns 198
elderflower, gooseberry & elderflower cupcakes 48
equipment 11
espresso cream cakes 178

F

festive spice cupcakes 214
figs, Christmas garland 204
filling the cases 13
firework sparklers 222
florentine cupcakes 164
flowers, frosted flower cupcakes 228
flying bats 218
football cupcakes 230
frangipane & apricot cupcakes 154
frosted blueberry cupcakes 158
frosted choc 'n' nut cupcakes 100
frosted flowers,
  frosted flower cupcakes 228
  wedding cupcakes 224
frosted fruit & flower cakes 226
frostings 18
fruit & nut cupcakes 24, 204
fruity flower cupcakes 132
fruity lunchbox muffins 120
fudge
  chocolate fudge cupcakes 70
  mini mint fudge cakes 152
funny clown cakes 128

G

ginger
  butter-iced ginger cupcakes 40
dark chocolate & ginger muffins 102
ginger spice Madeira cupcakes 168
iced fresh ginger cupcakes 146
mini simnel cakes 216
rich fruit chocolate cupcakes 92
snow-covered ginger buns 210
sultana & ginger cupcakes 40
gingerbread, iced gingerbread cupcakes 64
goat's cheese & tomato cakes 186
gooseberry & elderflower cupcakes 48
grapefruit, juniper & grapefruit muffins 32
grapes
  Christmas garland 204
  fruity flower cupcakes 132

H

hazelnuts
  courgette & hazelnut cupcakes 26
  frosted choc 'n' nut cupcakes 100
  orange & hazelnut drizzle cakes 34
  spiced apricot & hazelnut cupcakes 66
herbs, malted pepper & herb muffins 190
homemade caramel sauce 36
homemade vanilla sugar 100
honey & banana cakes 50
honey-drizzled spice cakes 222
hot & spicy cupcakes 146

I

iced fresh ginger cupcakes 146
iced gingerbread cupcakes 64
icing
  frostings 18
  making paper icing bags 16
  ready-to-roll 17
Indian spiced cornbreads 182

J

jelly bean cupcakes 122
jewelled bangle cupcakes 118
jewelled Christmas muffins 210
juniper & grapefruit muffins 32

L

ladybirds 110
lavender cupcakes 156
leek & Gruyère
  cupcakes 186
lemon
  citrus simnel cakes
    216
  daisy celebration
    cupcakes 232
  Easter chick & egg
    cakes 126
  Easter cupcakes
    214
  lemon & lime drizzle
    cupcakes 34
  lemon meringue
    cupcakes 176
  lemon swirl cupcakes
    122
  orange & lemon
    cupcakes 48
  poppy seed & lemon
    cupcakes 62
lentil cakes with
  crushed spices 194
lime
  coconut frosted cakes
    228
  lemon & lime drizzle
    cupcakes 34
liqueur-drizzled mocha
  cakes 178
little devils' cakes 134

M

macadamia & raspberry
  cupcakes 160
malted pepper & herb
  muffins 190
malty raisin cupcakes
  60
maple syrup
  maple & pecan
    praline cakes 148
  snow-covered ginger
    buns 210
  white chocolate maple
    muffins 102
marbled coffee
  cupcakes 28
marmalade Madeira
  cupcakes 168
marsala raisin & ricotta
  cakes 144
marshmallows,
  mile-high
  marshmallow
  cupcakes 56
melting chocolate 16
meringue
  lemon meringue
    cupcakes 176
  mini iced Alaskas
    176
microwave ovens,
  melting chocolate in
    17
mile-high marshmallow
  cupcakes 56
mincemeat cupcakes
  206
mini cheese & chive
  cakes 196
mini fruit parkins 64
mini iced Alaskas 176
mini linzer cakes 154
mini mint fudge cakes
  152
mini minted cupcakes
  152
mini simnel cakes
  216
mint
  mini minted cupcakes
    152
  mint chocolate
    cupcakes 90
  minted white
    chocolate cakes
    84
  peppermint tea &
    white chocolate
    muffins 162
mocha cupcakes
  94
muffin trays 11
muffins
  apple & sultana
    muffins 120
  corn, chilli & bacon
    muffins 182
  dark chocolate &
    ginger muffins
    102
  double berry muffins
    32
  fruity lunchbox
    muffins 120
  jewelled Christmas
    muffins 210
  juniper & grapefruit
    muffins 32
  making 13
  sweet camomile
    muffins 162
  white chocolate maple
    muffins 102
mushrooms, celeriac &
  mushroom muffins
    192

N

number cakes 140
nuts
  almond praline
    cupcakes 148
  Brazil nut & orange
    cupcakes 62
  breakfast fruit & nut
    cupcakes 66
  chocolate almond
    sandwich cakes 86
  chocolate fruit & nut
    cupcakes 72
  chocolate peanut
    cupcakes 80
  coffee & walnut
    cupcakes 170
  courgette & hazelnut
    cupcakes 26
  crunchy peanut
    cupcakes 170
  florentine cupcakes
    164
  frosted choc 'n' nut
    cupcakes 100
  fruit & nut cupcakes
    24, 204
  macadamia &
    raspberry cupcakes
    160
  orange & hazelnut
    drizzle cakes 34
  red pepper & pine nut
    cupcakes 184
  rich fruit chocolate
    cupcakes 92
  spiced apricot &
    hazelnut cupcakes
    66
  warm pecan caramel
    cupcakes 36

white chocolate maple muffins 102

O

olives, mini Parmesan & olive cakes 196
on the farm 114
onions, pumpkin & red onion cupcakes 194
orange
  Brazil nut & orange cupcakes 62
  chocolate jaffa cupcakes 80
  chocolate orange cupcakes 78
  citrus simnel cakes 216
  clementine cupcakes 112
  date & orange cupcakes 24
  orange & hazelnut drizzle cakes 34
  orange & lemon cupcakes 48–9

P

pancetta, Parmesan & pancetta cupcakes 188
paper icing bags, making 16
parkins, mini fruit 64
Parmesan & pancetta cupcakes 188
parsnips
  spicy cheese & parsnip muffins 192

spicy parsnip cakes 172
party 'name' cakes 140
passionfruit cream cupcakes 54
peach & redcurrant cupcakes 54
peanuts, chocolate peanut cupcakes 80
pears, spicy pear & goat's cheese cupcakes 166
pecan nuts, white chocolate maple muffins 102
peppermint tea & white chocolate muffins 162
peppers, red pepper & pine nut cupcakes 184
piña colada cupcakes 150
pine nuts, red pepper & pine nut cupcakes 184
pineapple
  fruity flower cupcakes 132
  pineapple & coconut cupcakes 58
  spicy pineapple cupcakes 44
pink coconut cupcakes 56
pink rose cupcakes 158
piped decorations 15
piped shell cupcakes 15, 30

pirate faces 128
pistachio cream cupcakes 160
plum polenta cupcakes 58
poppy seed & lemon cupcakes 62
potatoes, saffron & potato buns 200
princess cupcakes 118
prunes, chocolate prune cupcakes 78
pumpkin & red onion cupcakes 194
pumpkin heads 136

R

raisins
  breakfast fruit & nut cupcakes 66
  chocolate fruit & nut cupcakes 72
  chocolate, rum & raisin cupcakes 94
  malty raisin cupcakes 60
  marsala raisin & ricotta cakes 144
  rum & raisin cheesecakes 144
raspberries
  chocolate raspberry friands 96
  double berry muffins 32
  fruity flower cupcakes 132
  fruity lunchbox muffins 120

macadamia & raspberry cupcakes 160
raspberry amaretti cakes 174
raspberry oat crumble cupcakes 52
rippled raspberry cupcakes 28
ready-made decorations 17
ready-to-roll icing 17
red pepper & pine nut cupcakes 184
red velvet cupcakes 166
redcurrants, peach & redcurrant cupcakes 54
reindeer cupcakes 130
rhubarb crumble cupcakes 52
rich fruit chocolate cupcakes 92
rippled raspberry cupcakes 28
rose delight cupcakes 42
rosemary, chorizo & rosemary cupcakes 188
rum
  chocolate, rum & raisin cupcakes 94
  rum & raisin cheesecakes 144
rye & caraway buns 198

S

saffron & potato buns 200

silicone cases 11
simnel cakes 216
sleepy puppies 124
smoked salmon cakes 190
snakes in the jungle 106
snow-covered ginger buns 210
spiced apricot & hazelnut cupcakes 66
spiced sweet potato cupcakes 172
spicy cheese & parsnip muffins 192
spicy parsnip cakes 172
spicy pear & goat's cheese cupcakes 166
spicy pineapple cupcakes 44
sponge, making basic 12
spooky spider cakes 218
stands for cupcakes 8, 9, 12
star & moon cupcakes 220
stars, spots & stripes 220
storing cupcakes 12
strawberries
  chocolate strawberry cupcakes 86
  fruity lunchbox muffins 12
  strawberry cream cupcakes 38
  strawberry cupcakes 132

strawberry marguerita cupcakes 150
sugar
  homemade vanilla sugar 100
  sugar-dusted rose cupcakes 42
sultanas
  apple & sultana muffins 120
  florentine cupcakes 164
  sultana & ginger cupcakes 40
  sweet camomile muffins 162
sweet camomile muffins 162
sweet potatoes, spiced sweet potato cupcakes 172
sweet thyme cupcakes 156
sweetheart cupcakes 30

T
tee-off cakes 230
testing if cakes are cooked 15
thyme, sweet thyme cupcakes 156
toffee
  chocolate toffee cupcakes 90
  toffee crunch cupcakes 164
tomatoes, goat's cheese & tomato cakes 186

triple chocolate cupcakes 82
tumbling number cakes 108

V
valentine hearts 226
vanilla
  daisy celebration cupcakes 232
  homemade vanilla sugar 100
  vanilla cupcakes 22
  vanilla custard butterfly cupcakes 46
very cherry cupcakes 44

W
walnuts
  chocolate fruit & nut cupcakes 72
  coffee & walnut cupcakes 15, 170
warm chocolate brownie cakes 88
warm pecan caramel cupcakes 36
wedding cupcakes 8, 224
white chocolate
  alphabetti cupcakes 108
  chocolate blondie cupcakes 88
  chocolate coconut kisses 76
  chocolate honeycomb cheesecakes 74

daisy celebration cupcakes 232
  frosted choc 'n' nut cupcakes 100
  frosted flower cupcakes 228
  mini mint fudge cakes 152
  minted white chocolate cakes 84
  peppermint tea & white chocolate muffins 162
  triple chocolate cupcakes 82
  white chocolate blueberry friands 96
  white chocolate curl cakes 76
  white chocolate frosting 18
  white chocolate fudge cakes 70
  white chocolate maple muffins 102
  white-chocolate-frosted cardamom cakes 84
wiggly worms 116
winter wonderland cakes 208

Y
yoghurt
  clementine cupcakes 112
  frosted banana cupcakes 112
  yoghurt & banana cakes 50

acknowledgements

Executive Editor: Eleanor Maxfield
Senior Editor: Lisa John
Deputy Creative Director: Karen Sawyer
Designer: Geoff Fennell
Photographer: David Munns
Home Economist: Joanna Farrow
Props Stylist: Liz Hippisley
Production Controller: Carolin Stransky

Special photography: © Octopus Publishing Group Limited/David Munns.
Other photography: © Octopus Publishing Group Limited 20; /Stephen Conroy 16 right, 123; /Vanessa Davies 33, 135, 137; /David Munns 68, 142, 180, 202; /Lis Parsons 49, 131, 211; /Gareth Sambidge 8, 25, 31, 39, 46, 71, 77, 83, 91, 101, 107, 111, 115, 119, 127, 141, 165, 179, 205, 209, 213, 219, 221, 225, 227, 231; /Ian Wallace 16 left, 95, 103.